Ethical Leadership

Rebuilding Trust in Corporations

Second Edition

Richard Bellingham, Ed.D.

HRD Press Inc. • Amherst • Massachusetts

HRD Press, Inc.
22 Amherst Road
Amherst, MA 01002-9709
800-822-2801 (U.S. and Canada)
413-253-3488
413-253-3490 (Fax)
www.hrdpress.com

Ethical Leadership, Second Edition

Editorial Services: Mary George

Cover Designer: Eileen Klockars

10 9 8 7 6 5 4 3 2 1

ISBN 0-87425-738-7

Contents

Foreword Ethics in America:
An Essential Pursuit

Who can you trust? For many Americans today, the answer is deeply influenced by staggering examples of wrongdoing by corporations, politicians, and religious leaders.

There is a deepening vein of public mistrust and skepticism about our public institutions and the people who run them. Corporate America has lost credibility as the greed, vanity, and manipulation of a few prominent CEOs becomes known. Political candidates savage one another with half-truths or outright lies, gaining office in the wake of diminishing public participation in the political process. Financial-services firms portray their competitors as self-serving and inept, damaging consumer faith in their own industry in the process.

We live in a social environment that challenges ethical behavior. Americans value individualism and economic success. Self-interest is a virtue. Short-term profit and quarterly results take precedence over the long haul. Doing the right thing is often compromised in an attempt to avoid litigation, navigate through a sea of regulation, or manipulate customers. Wall Street devalues employees as overhead when announced staff reductions push up a company's stock price.

There is a better way to manage our personal lives, our companies, and our public institutions. Dr. Bellingham provides a convincing argument that strong ethical standards and adherence to clear values and responsible norms can provide corporations with a strategic competitive advantage and enrich us as employers, family members, and community citizens.

His philosophy of ethical leadership has profoundly influenced my approach to business, initially as managing partner and co-owner of a private mortgage banking company, and later as president of a public real estate investment firm's national commercial mortgage subsidiary.

I have learned how essential it is to trust *and* to be trusted. I have shared in the profound rewards of honest and forthright dialogue with fellow employees, customers, and stockholders. I have seen employees coalesce into an energized, focused, and highly successful team when they understand the company's vision and their role in achieving it.

The pages that follow provide insights into ethical leadership, values, and culture that have been an integral part of Dr. Bellingham's philosophy since I first met him nearly 20 years ago. They are concepts that have been fired in the heat of a changing, evolving corporate America.

Strong, visible leadership, clearly articulated values, and a consistent vision could help to overcome the malaise we find in our society today. Dr. Bellingham provides a roadmap to get there.

T. Michael Forney, CMB
President, PW Funding, Inc.
Mineola, New York

Preface

Ethical leadership comes down to putting others above yourself. And that is where we are failing.

The first edition of this book was published in 1987, when greed was still in its relative infancy and millionaires were still relatively rare. It thus preceded the economic boom of the 1990s, a decade in which market values escalated to outrageous levels, millionaires multiplied by the thousands, and accounting irregularities were fairly rare or largely ignored. Recruiting top talent and fighting off venture capitalists seemed the biggest problems that corporate executives faced. Then came September 11 and, in its wake, a raft of Chapter 11s. The world changed. However, the principles espoused in the 1987 edition, so valid then, became even more valid. We perhaps need them now more than ever.

For over 20 years, I have explored the principles of ethical leadership and observed the practices of corporate leaders. I have worked in the trenches where decisions get made. In my interactions with thousands of leaders over time, I have found the vast majority to be good, honest people who take care to do the right thing. There are, of course, those who are greedy. Many are too driven by self-interest, and some are insufferable with their narcissism. Few are capable of creating the disasters we see unfolding before us, yet those few can and have caused serious damage. They have brought about a serious breach of trust and a shocking sense of vulnerability that, in turn, have created a need to restore trust in corporate America. In essence, this book is about rebuilding that trust, so badly damaged in the first years of our new millennium.

To begin to repair this situation, we must realize that corporations have the dual challenge of growing *revenues* and *relationships*. In this respect, although the economic, political, and social contexts have changed, my message today is the same as it was in 1987: focusing on either one—revenues or relationships—at the expense of the other has proved and will prove disastrous. In the 1990s, corporations became obsessed with market valuations and took their eyes off both revenues and relationships. Now corporate leaders need to focus their energies, invest in the relationships that will enable their organizations to succeed, and provide revenue reports that investors can trust.

This second edition proceeds from my firm belief that corporations must commit to what is important and what is fundamental for success: a dual focus on revenues and relationships. Because many corporations have abused the trust of customers, employees, and investors in recent years, that trust will be hard to rebuild. It can only be done with patience, commitment, and honest dealings. It can only be done through ethical leadership. This book provides a roadmap, focusing on relationships—with employees, customers, investors, partners, and communities—that lead to increasing revenue and profitability, as well as renewed trust.

WAKE-UP CALLS

For this book to have any real meaning to you, it is important that you have some level of relationship to me. Thus allow me to share several experiences— "wake-up calls"—that will give you a better sense of my perspective and history. They touch on my role in helping companies improve both revenues and relationships, and reflect my motivations for writing this book.

The first wake-up call came in 1968, in Vietnam, when I was serving a one-year term in Saigon as a military intelligence operative for the U.S. Army. I had enlisted in military intelligence on the promise of a year of German language training in the States and then a two-year tour of duty in Germany. As an international marketing major about to be drafted into the infantry, I considered this to be a good deal. Six months later, I was in Vietnam. There I came face to face with the process of dehumanizing people and its effects. Basically, if a whole population of people can be reduced to a label like "gooks," then their lives become meaningless and you can kill with impunity. This taught me a simple but crucial lesson: labels distort and limit our ability to relate to people as unique human beings.

A second wake-up call came in 1972 when I served as director of a jail rehabilitation program in Kalamazoo, Michigan. I was responsible for providing inmates with the skills and support they required to preclude repeated incarceration. A critical success factor in the program—which, over three years, reduced recidivism by 50 percent—was interpersonal-skills training for inmates and correctional officers. We found that interpersonal communication was a far more effective weapon than hoses and clubs. Before the program, the county had spent over a million dollars cleaning up the facility after years of trashing by inmates. With basic training of correctional officers and a token economy system, we reduced clean-up costs to practically nothing. I learned that even under the harshest conditions, constructive relationships can make a difference, including one's relationship with the community. Indeed, for us, the latter had been the most important factor to take into account. Linking up employees with community resources provided ex-inmates with the support they needed to sustain changes in their behavior made possible through intensive skills training.

A third wake-up call came in 1984 when I served as a consultant for AT&T. "Ma Bell" was trying to transform herself from a monopoly with more than one million employees to a deregulated entrepreneurial organization with 300 thousand employees. I had formed an organizational-effectiveness consulting firm, Possibilities, Inc., and was retained as a consultant on the managing-change committee. The committee's primary charge was to minimize the adverse effects of change and to help employees see change as an opportunity. One of the major programs that came out of the committee was a comprehensive wellness program called Total Life Concept (TLC). TLC contributed significantly to employee satisfaction during those turbulent times and helped to change the employer-employee relationship at AT&T. As a result of a rigorous evaluation study, the company projected cost savings of more than 300 million dollars over a 10-year period from a reduction of health risks attributed to TLC. This experience taught me that, in addition to lifestyle behaviors, the norms and values of the worksite could have a powerful impact not only on quality of life but on longevity as well. The relationship between employer and employee made a significant difference.

The last wake-up call I will share came in 1995 at Lotus/IBM. I had served as a consultant to Lotus executives for several years before IBM announced its hostile take-over bid. Since I had consulted on several mergers and acquisitions and had formed close relationships with most of the Lotus team, Russ Campanello, the senior vice president of Human Resources, asked me to be the primary consultant on the integration. This effort was a study in demographic differences. The Lotus culture could be described as young, creative, freewheeling, and energetic. The IBM culture, from the Lotus point of view, could be described as old, stodgy, rigid, and boring. Bringing these cultures together required extensive dialogue between functional representatives from both companies. We formed integration teams for sales, services, marketing, human resources, legal affairs, finance, information management, and technology. I learned that successful mergers and transformation efforts require respecting differences in cultural norms and values and that meaningful involvement from all functions is required before decisions can be made that all parties will support.

The theme of all these wake-up calls is that *relationship is the most important success factor in any venture.* This is true independent of the goal. If the goal is to reduce tensions, it is essential to build relationships with a broad coalition of partners. If the goal is to improve trust, it is critical to develop positive relationships with the people whose trust you want and need. If the goal is to increase revenues, it is necessary to build productive relationships with customers, partners, employees, and communities.

I was CEO of Possibilities, Inc., for 20 years and never suffered a loss. I also have worked with more than 200 companies helping them to increase revenues and improve relationships. I thus know this book can be a wake-up call *to you* that will result not only in higher revenues but also in more satisfying and enduring relationships.

THE ISSUE OF ETHICS

This book positions ethics as a competitive edge and challenges the assumption that ethics and profitability are unrelated. It also challenges leaders to respond to new ethical issues as moral and business opportunities. By doing so, leaders will develop an organizational culture that thrives *because* it is ethical.

Increasingly, contemporary organizations realize that ethics and profits are not conflicting concerns. As awareness grows about the relationship between ethical leadership and competitive advantage, corporations are emphasizing one or another aspect of ethics (for example, environment). Yet gaining a real competitive edge requires comprehensive ethical leadership, including people, customers, and communities. Top executives note that good ethics is a prime corporate asset. They understand that a solid ethical foundation is one of the important components for long-term corporate success.[1]

Defining Ethics

We define ethics in a twofold manner as:

- The discipline of dealing with what is good and bad, and with moral duty and obligation;

- The principles of conduct governing an individual or a group.[2]

At its core, ethics involves the discipline of decency. And the essence of ethics is interdependent thinking and questioning.[3]

Business ethics is deeply concerned with both moral values and moral actions. Moral values are basic ideals that are considered desirable or worthwhile for human interaction. Moral actions are the overt expressions and applications of these underlying values. Therefore, the notion that, as businesspersons, we should not deceive or mislead our customers is a moral value. Behaving honestly and fairly toward our customers is a moral action. Business ethics is called into question when the moral values or the accompanying moral actions of organizational decision-makers conflict with the commonly accepted standards of society.[4]

The Ethics Grid

The fundamental issues related to ethical leadership can be categorized in the Ethics Grid, shown in Figure 1.

	ETHICS	
BUSINESS	Good	Bad
Good		
Bad		

Figure 1. The Ethics Grid

Decisions that fall into the Good/Good or the Bad/Bad cells tend to be easy to make. After all, why wouldn't leaders support decisions that make good business sense and are highly ethical? And for all those decisions that are highly unethical and make for bad business, voting no would also be a simple matter. Yet recent decisions by WorldCom, Xerox, and Enron would lead one to wonder. When leaders fail to make the right choices, such as paying employees fairly (Good/Good) or dumping garbage on a main street (Bad/Bad), the poor choice can be attributed politely to unenlightened thinking or — not so politely — to stupidity. I guess it's not so surprising that Michael Moore's new book, *Stupid White Men,* topped the best-seller list in 2002 and 2003.

On the other hand, those issues that fall into the Good/Bad or the Bad/Good cells present an entirely different challenge. This gray area is where many executives wallow in ethical ambiguity. Exploring such areas is a powerful way to identify sticky issues and to probe more deeply the ethical implications for the company. Taking a "deep dive" into grey areas usually results in a much clearer image of how a company defines itself. Taking a hard look at issues that seem easier to ignore can help companies make the right decisions.

In terms of the Ethics Grid, this book will demonstrate that:

- More opportunities exist in the Good/Good mode than we realize.

- Few companies that operate in the Good Business/Bad Ethics mode succeed over the long term.

- More understanding is needed for the hard choices that exist in the Good Ethics/Bad Business mode.

The Ethical Leader

There is more than enlightened self-interest at work among leaders who conform to rigorous ethical guidelines and pressures. What really motivates them is an interest in developing ethical attitudes toward living, learning, and working. When it appears that the market will respond favorably to apparent changes in ethical behaviors, the ethical leader is more concerned that ethical values dominate management thinking. He or she understands these two critical principles:

1. Ethical initiatives that come entirely from a "business" perspective may have temporary effects, but will erode when business pressures or market data demand a change in strategy.

2. If ethical initiatives originate for ethical reasons, then changes will be more lasting and will be less influenced by market manipulation.

The ethical leader knows that a true change in business ethics requires a frontal assault on who we are, not just token efforts to increase knowledge about what one can and cannot do according to a code of ethics. At its most basic level, the ethical leader thinks about *others*.

As for codes of ethics, in many corporations they have had little impact on employee actions. This is largely because they have sought only to protect firms from the actions of their employees and have stressed "legalese"; most codes have neglected the important ethical issues related to culture, environment, people, customers, and communities.[5] There is no real power in pushing codes—that is, there is no dynamic growth in codes. Instead, ethical growth usually emerges as a result of meaningful dialogue about tough issues. Ethical leaders are willing to pursue and engage in such dialogue.

The Ethical Leadership Scale

This book encourages readers who hold any position of leadership to consider the personal principles on which they base their decisions. It is designed to help them assess the current level of ethical functioning in their organizations and to explore how they can gain competitive advantage by developing an "ethical edge." Throughout the book, variations of the Ethical Leadership Scale, shown below, are provided to facilitate this approach. Here it appears in its basic form, to help leaders determine, in a general way, their current level of ethical functioning, and to prompt them to decide what their goal is in relation to ethics.

THE ETHICAL LEADERSHIP SCALE

5.0 Ethical Exemplar

4.0 Ethical Culture

3.0 Ethical Leadership

2.0 Compliance with Internal and External Laws and Regulations

1.0 Ethical Minimum—Stay Out of Trouble

The premise of this book is that a level-four or level-five goal is required to turn an ethical burden into a competitive edge, and exemplary leadership is required to achieve that edge. Ethical leadership is more than complying with legal regulations and accounting standards. It is *setting the standard for principle-driven relationships*. Exemplars provide us with a model of how leadership can create an ethical culture. These are leaders who, by their example, buttress the assertion that trust can be rebuilt in corporations.

OVERVIEW OF THE BOOK

Ethical Leadership is composed of five chapters. A summary of their contents follows:

- **Chapter 1, "Creating an Ethical Culture,"** addresses the relationship of ethics to corporate culture. It shows how vision, values, and norms are the critical ingredients in any approach to organizational change related to ethics. Envisioning what is possible and articulating core values serve as guideposts for making ethical decisions along the way.

- **Chapter 2, "Winning through People,"** addresses company-employee relationships. The topics here include the principles of developing people, promoting health and safety, creating a sense of balance, and valuing differences. Relating constructively with employees is the starting point for building an ethical culture. It sets the tone for all relationships.

- **Chapter 3, "Winning with Customers,"** addresses the ethical considerations of customer relationships. It addresses principles related to product development, manufacturing, and marketing. The way a company relates to customers not only defines who it is as a company but also has a major impact on profitability over the long term.

- **Chapter 4, "Winning for the Community,"** discusses ways in which organizations deal with the communities in which they are located. The topics here include enhancing the environment, contributing to community resources, and participating in community organizations. Socially responsible companies build trust among their constituents and, as a result, build healthy balance sheets over time.

- **Chapter 5, "Action Steps and Strategies,"** provides action steps for the ethical leader. It suggests strategies for transforming principles into action. These actions are a measure of the integrity of the firm. They constitute the day-to-day behaviors that lead investors and stakeholders to trust the information provided by the firm for them to make their own buying decisions, employment decisions, regulatory decisions, and investment decisions.

Chapters 1 through 4 are each divided into five parts: an introduction, overview, issues section, exemplars section, and challenge. These give the reader a general idea of how the material can contribute to competitive advantage; they also provide a rationale for taking action, and demonstrate what other companies have done to enhance their profitability through exemplary ethics.

In addition, rating scales for each area are included in the overview section, so that decision-makers can assess the current ethical status of their companies. The appendix offers a more integrated ethics assessment and goal-setting tool, and readers are encouraged to use this tool to monitor their progress when putting ethical leadership into action.

IN SUMMARY

Organizations need to take a hard look at the way they do business, and decide what changes are required. They need to understand explicitly the issues related to ethical behavior now and in the future. Leaders need to have a vision of how ethics can create new possibilities for the future growth of the business, and must understand what steps they can take to lay the groundwork for connecting ethics and traditional strategy in every phase of the business. It is my hope that this book will help organizations and leaders meet these needs in an ethical and profitable fashion.

REFERENCES

1. Stoner, C. R. "The Foundations of Business Ethics: Exploring the Relationship between Organizational Culture, Moral Values, and Actions." *Advanced Management Journal,* Summer, 1989.
2. *Merriam-Webster's Collegiate Dictionary,* 10th edition. Springfield, Mass.: Merriam-Webster, Inc., 1993.
3. Pastin, M. *The Hard Problems of Management: Gaining the Ethics Edge.* San Francisco: Jossey-Bass, 1986.
4. Stoner, C. R. "The Foundations of Business Ethics."
5. Matthews, M. "Corporate Ethical Codes," in *Research in Corporate Social Performance and Policy,* vol. 9, W. E. Frederick, ed. Greenwich, Connecticut: JAI Press, 1987.

Introduction

There are two outstanding problems with the world economy: too much terror and too little trust. We can't do much about the first, but we can do a lot about the second.

The events of September 11, 2001 and the threat of further terrorist attacks have made people around the world skittish and anxious. Investors know that another attack will send markets worldwide into a tailspin. As a result, many people are staying on the sidelines or investing in real estate. The mass shift from participant to observer has made growth more difficult.

Trust is another issue. Reports from organizations such as WorldCom, IM Clone, Vivendi, Global Crossing, Lucent, Adelphia, Microsoft, Tyco, Xerox, Enron, and Arthur Andersen have made investors suspicious about the real health of some of the world's most recognized corporations. Investors are reluctant to pour savings into companies where too many unknowns exist.

These two problems have made investments a treacherous proposition and management a perilous journey. Never before has it been so necessary for ethical leadership to navigate the economic sea. And as more cases of unethical conduct come to light, CEOs are put under closer and closer scrutiny.

"NIGHTMARES" — AND THE CURE

The worst nightmare of any CEO is to be exposed for unethical behavior. It doesn't bode well for family relationships or country club status. In the last decade, many CEOs have had their share of nightmares. Unfortunately, most were well deserved. Here are three examples that ushered in the new millennium.

Nightmare 1: A Subpoena from the Federal Government

Following are extracts from a letter from House Energy and Commerce Committee Chairman Billy Tauzin to Enron Chairman Kenneth Lay:

January 14, 2002
Dear Mr. Lay:

As you know, the Committee on Energy and Commerce is investigating matters relating to the financial collapse of the Enron Corporation ("Enron"). As part of this investigation, the Committee requested and received thousands of pages of documents from Enron, its auditing firm, Andersen, and other individuals involved with Enron. During the course of reviewing these documents, Committee investigators uncovered an Enron document that raises troubling questions about the extent to which you and other senior officials at Enron and Andersen were aware of the controversial financial transactions and accounting practices that would ultimately contribute significantly to Enron's demise. The Committee's investigation also uncovered that Enron requested and received a legal review of such matters dated October 15, 2001 — one day before Enron announced its third-quarter earnings and the $1.2 billion reduction in shareholder equity due to losses later associated with various partnerships involving Enron officials.

Specifically, in August 2001, a knowledgeable Enron employee wrote a letter to you as Enron's chairman and chief executive officer, questioning the propriety of Enron's accounting treatment of certain "related party" transactions and deconsolidated "special purpose entities." In that letter, the employee identified several areas of concern.

The employee described a "veil of secrecy around LJM and Raptor," and noted that several senior Enron employees "consistently and constantly" questioned the corporation's accounting methods to senior Enron officials, and directly to Jeffrey Skilling — Enron's former Chief Executive Officer — regarding the LJM transactions. "It sure looks to the layman on the street that we are hiding losses in a related company and will compensate that company with Enron stock in the future."

In order for the Committee to gain a more complete understanding of the events surrounding this particular matter, we are requesting that, pursuant to Rules X and XI of the U.S. House of Representatives, Enron produce to the Committee the following information by January 28, 2002:

1. All records relating to any investigation or review of the allegations raised by the Enron employee in August 2001, including but not limited to the review done by Vinson & Elkins at Enron's request and any internal Andersen or Enron review.

2. The names of all Enron employees who were interviewed, participated in, or from whom any information was requested, as part of any investigation or review referenced in Request No. 1.

Thank you for your prompt attention to these matters. We appreciate your continuing cooperation with our investigation.

Nightmare 2: A Wall Street Journal Exposé

The following is reprinted with permission from The Wall Street Journal. *It was written by staff reporters Laurie P. Cohen and Mark Maremont.*

New York investigators are examining a wide range of expenses by Tyco International Ltd. related to the company's relocation of employees to Florida, including whether company funds were used to purchase a Boca Raton house from a director and whether the company offered interest-free mortgages to many employees, people familiar with the matter said. Among the questions being asked by investigators is whether any New York state or federal securities laws were broken by some of the dealings, including whether the purchase of the Boca Raton home should have been disclosed to shareholders as a "related party" transaction.

The questions are part of a widening investigation into Tyco and its just-departed chief executive, L. Dennis Kozlowski, who was indicted last week on charges that he evaded sales tax on $13.2 million in art purchased using funds borrowed from Tyco. In addition, New York investigators are looking into the purchase of an $18 million Manhattan apartment in Mr. Kozlowski's name, using what a person close to Tyco's board said were company funds. Mr. Kozlowski has pleaded not guilty to the tax-evasion charges.

Investigators have been especially intrigued by the circuitous ownership record involving the Boca Raton house once owned by director Michael A. Ashcroft, at the exclusive Royal Palm Yacht and Country Club. Mr. Ashcroft is a British-born tycoon who joined Tyco's board in July 1997 when his security-alarm firm, ADT Ltd., merged with Tyco. In October 1997, the house was sold by Mr. Ashcroft to his wife for $100, who then sold it the same day for $2.5 million to Byron S. Kalogerou, a Tyco vice president, Florida property records show.

Although officially based in Bermuda, Tyco has long had U.S. headquarters in Exeter, N.H., in an unassuming building held up as a symbol of the company's leanness. But after Tyco merged with ADT in 1997, Mr. Kozlowski began spending more time at ADT's headquarters in Boca Raton, people close to the company said. Mr. Kozlowski is listed as the owner of a 15,000 square-foot mansion in Boca Raton, bought for $10.6 million last year.

Nightmare 3: From Ethical Exemplar to Greedy Goon

The following is reprinted with permission from The Wall Street Journal. *It was written by staff reporters Ken Brown and Ianthe Jeanne Dugan.*

At "Andersen U.," the lush, 150-acre campus where Arthur Andersen LLP has trained tens of thousands of new recruits, there's a shrine to ethical accounting.

A display in the Andersen Heritage Center is devoted to yellowing press clippings of a long-ago campaign to clean up the accounting industry by Leonard Spacek, who led the firm from 1947 to 1963. In one, he accused Bethlehem Steel of overstating its profits in 1964 by more than 60%. In another, he bashed the Securities and Exchange Commission for failing to crack down on companies that cooked their books, saying that at best the regulatory agency has been "a brake on the rate of retrogression in the quality of accounting."

Now, it's the quality of Andersen's accounting that has set off an ethical crisis. Since 1993, the firm has been embroiled in a series of major accounting scandals—from Sunbeam Corp. to Waste Management Inc. to Enron Corp. Facing an obstruction-of-justice charge in a Houston federal court, Andersen itself is disintegrating and will likely be gone in a matter of months regardless of the verdict—a humiliating end to a company that once stood as the world's largest professional-services firm and whose 85,000 employees last year generated $9.3 billion in revenue.

Andersen's descent from conscience of the accounting industry to accused felon didn't happen overnight. Rather, it stemmed from a series of management miscues and compromises over the decades. As the firm grew from a close-knit partnership to a globe-spanning behemoth, pressure to boost profits became intense. Andersen leaders responded by pushing partners to become salesmen—upsetting the delicate balancing act any auditor must perform between pleasing a client and looking out for the public investor.

It's time to wake up and end the nightmares—to realize that *ethical leadership is an essential part of the cure*. We may need some legislative changes, but what we really need are cultural changes.

With this in mind, let me emphasize that my purpose here is not to keep unethical executives out of jail, but to inspire leaders to elevate the level of their relationships with stakeholders and key constituents. Again, such relationships are critical to the success of any organization. In terms made clear by Dr. Robert R. Carkhuff, they constitute the DNA of marketplace capital, organizational capital, human capital, information capital, and mechanical capital—the "new capital development" ingredients that will fuel economic growth in the future.[1] Accordingly, this book provides understandable ways to audit ethical behavior and to elevate those relationship levels. It prompts us to start thinking anew about *how to do well by doing good* and, I hope, guides us toward the cure by offering real solutions to the problem.

Best Practices: Interdependence and Community

Based on an extensive review of the literature since 1987 (see Appendix B), it appears that the best practices for ethical leadership are the following:

- Challenge processes.
- Encourage the heart.
- Strive for consistency and congruence.
- Think long-term.
- Look at the whole.
- Tap employees' commitment and capacity to learn.
- Share power.
- Ensure diversity of voices.
- Create a humane and nurturing workplace.
- Build interdependent relationships.
- Foster community.
- Accept ownership and accountability.
- Resist policies of self-interest.
- Put people and creativity at the center.
- Be authentic.
- Engage in constructive collaboration.
- Develop stories of integrity.
- Create a culture of trust.

Why are these practices so difficult to institutionalize? The simple answer is that we are fighting history and habits. We live in a culture that values independence and supports an economic system built on self-interest. These best practices, however, require interdependent thinking and a focus on community. In many ways, they are countercultural. It is thus no surprise that they are not the accepted, expected, and reinforced behaviors in organizational cultures.

Interdependence and community bring us once again to the vital importance of relationship. Indeed, we may say that *building interdependent relationships forms the core of ethical leadership.* All of these best practices can be seen as subsets of this critical element. It is a primary reason why this book focuses on building relationships—interdependent relationships—with employees, customers, partners, and communities.

CHANGING TIMES: A REVIEW

Some organizations have taken a defensive posture in relation to ethical issues. They see new developments in ethical awareness as a threat to the status quo. Many others, however, are taking a proactive stance to make sure that they are doing the right things, and to benefit from improvements in employee and customer relations. Ethical standards have changed rapidly over the past decade or so and the rate of change is increasing. A review of these changes, including the advantages they offer and the exemplars supporting it, gives us a sense of how dramatic they are.

We begin with essayist Myron Magnet, who in 1987 observed that "as if trapped by a thermal inversion, the ethical atmosphere of business is growing acrid and the inhalation of those pernicious vapors could only lead to ever worse behavior."[2] If that observation had any truth to it, then how could the process be turned around?

John Shad, a former vice-chairman of E. F. Hutton and past chairman of the Securities and Exchange Commission, pledged $30 million to the Harvard Business School to try to find the answer. His gift was for the promotion and study of business ethics. From his close association with the finance community, Shad publicly declared his disgust with market malfeasance. He had strong feelings about how business ought to be done. And one of the things he got for his remarkable contribution was a public forum in which to air his conviction that "ethics pays," and "the marketplace does reward integrity."[3]

It seems Shad's premise has validity. An analysis of 15 *Fortune* 500 companies in operation for at least 30 years found that the companies that had maintained two things — (1) a written set of principles specifying the company's public service policy, and (2) an adherence to those principles for at least a generation — had, over a 30-year period ending in 1982, an average growth in profits of 11 percent. In a roughly comparable period, the balance of these companies experienced a growth rate in profits of 6.1 percent.[4] We may say, therefore, that the study indicates that ethical leadership very likely does provide a competitive edge in business. As a matter of note, this book explains why and enables organizations to determine how they can win the right way.

Participating in global markets increasingly requires that host countries be satisfied that foreign investors are sensitive to their concerns. More and more often, North American-based multinationals are finding that countries elsewhere insist that businesses act responsibly toward people, communities, stakeholders, and customers. Ethical sensitivities are not, after all, restricted to North America. Countries around the world are growing more concerned about their environment, the health and safety of their people, and the ways in which business is conducted, and so they are demanding appropriate behavior from global companies.

To bolster this movement, North American consumers, not just foreign governments, are disturbed by the implications of looming environmental problems abroad, such as the depletion of the ozone layer, global warming, and the destruction of the Brazilian rain forest. These consumers are also focusing their impatience for progress on the North American companies perceived to be implicated in environmental problems occurring offshore. North American governments, in turn, are applying similarly tough standards on foreign-based companies doing business here, such as Japanese forest-products companies operating in Alberta, Canada.

These changes have profound implications for the modern corporation. They represent tremendous potential for those companies who act now to seize the advantage. Some companies, of course, already have. James E. Burke, retired chairman of Johnson & Johnson, Inc., states that "There's an important correlation between a corporation's public responsibility and its ultimate financial performance. Although public service is implied in the charter of all American companies, public responsibility, in reality, is a company's very reason for existing." This perspective reveals Burke to be what we call an *ethics exemplar*. We will find similar exemplars in the balance of this book.

Using the principles of ethical leadership as a vehicle for competitive advantage represents an overlooked opportunity for most firms. This opportunity can be a significant source of gain for innovative companies, and go a long way toward increasing productivity as well.

Leaders have been dealing with ethical issues since their inception. Several factors have influenced how the scope and nature of these issues have changed.

- First, the ownership of businesses has changed from single owner-operators living in the host community to a heterogeneous group of stakeholders living all over the world who may know very little about the company or the communities in which the business operates.

- Second, the philosophy of running a business has changed from a small-town, homespun notion that "the business operates in the interest of society" to a legalistic, compliance mentality that "action must be legally and morally acceptable."

- Third, locations of businesses have changed from local manufacturing plants to international service and manufacturing networks.

- Finally, control of the way businesses are run has changed. Influence has shifted from personal values to heavy governmental regulation. Union and professional codes of ethics exert a powerful influence.[5]

In short, there has been an insidious breakdown of connectedness between businesses and the communities in which they reside. This itself will change because it must.

In the new millennium, we will see an even more rapid evolution of corporate ethics. Corporate ownership will be by international stakeholders. Not only will corporate constituents represent every area of the world, they will also be concerned with how the policies and actions of a particular company may affect their part of the planet. Corporate philosophy will become "You have to do good to do well." The realization will occur that employment and purchasing decisions are largely influenced by the perceived ethics of the company. Companies will be located all over the world as global markets expand. Goods and services will be produced and provided wherever it makes the most sense to do so.

Finally, the driving values for doing business will be international cooperation and interdependence. Universal connectedness will become more of a reality as the Internet creates a world community. People will realize that actions cannot be seen in isolation.

TABLE 1. The Evolution of Business

	Ownership	Ethics	Location	Control
PHASE I Before 1800	Single owner living in community	Business operates in the interest of society	Local	Individual values
PHASE II 1800-1900	Close-knit shareholders living near community	Business is interested in society	Regional	Community values
PHASE III 1900-1950	Homo-geneous shareholders living in same country	What's good for business is good for country	National	Some governmental and union values
PHASE IV 1950-2000	Hetero-geneous stakeholders living throughout world	Action must be morally and legally acceptable	Multi-national	Professional and corporate codes of ethics
PHASE V 2000 +	International stakeholders	You have to do good to do well	Global	International cooperation and inter-dependence

   Table 2 summarizes how these factors have changed over time, and projects what business can expect in the years to come.

THE NEED FOR A PROACTIVE APPROACH

While ethics awareness is growing, most of the discussion revolves around avoidance issues: loss of consumer confidence, potential for fines, pressure from special interest

groups, legal and financial vulnerability of corporate executives and professionals, and increasing attention to pollution
and negative publicity. Corporations thus are saying they
want to stay out of trouble and be in compliance with the law
so that they do not lose consumer confidence, get fined, come
under pressure from special interest groups, get thrown in jail,
be seen as a polluter, or suffer negative exposure in the media.

There tends to be minimal discussion on proactive issues.
For example, how can we increase our competitive advantage
through an ethical approach? How can we restore trust with
our shareholders? The emphasis is on constraints and obliga-
tions rather than opportunities and possibilities, the latter of
which this book addresses.

In conclusion, it should be noted that the current social
environment does not support a more proactive approach.
There is a corporate paranoia stemming from litigious
exploitation of system imperfections. Thus, an inordinate
amount of corporate energy is directed toward the avoidance
of problems rather than the creation of systematic solutions. In
order to create an ethical culture, leaders need to take a proactive approach to identifying ethical issues, engaging in meaningful dialogue about the right course of action for their
companies, and clarifying the values and principles that
anchor all decision making. This book provides the framework for ethical leaders to take a proactive approach toward
restoring public trust in corporations. It is a thinking tool for
elevating relationships with customers, employers, and communities. Most important, this book suggests practical ideas
for creating an ethical culture in corporations—a culture that
capitalizes on possibilities instead of capitulating to problems.

REFERENCES

1. Carkhuff, R. R. *The Age of the New Capitalism.* Amherst, Massachusetts:
   HRD Press, 1988.

2. Magnet, M. "The Money Society." *Fortune,* July 9, 1987.
3. Shames, L. *The Hunger for More: Searching for Values in an Age of Greed.* Times Books: New York, 1989.
4. Brooks, L. J. "Corporate Codes of Ethics." *Journal of Business Ethics,* 1989.
5. Ibid.

1

Creating an Ethical Culture

INTRODUCTION

An ethical corporate culture is one in which the vision of the organization includes its employees, its customers, and the community. The organization's values and norms support actions consistent with an ethical vision. The ethical perspective is so embedded in how the organization does business that no major business decision is made without the consideration of its impact on employees, customers, and the community. Before we explore how to create such a culture, some discussion of concepts and classifications would be helpful.

Primary among the concepts essential to our task are the following:

- **Organizational culture** — the unseen, unwritten, and unobservable force always behind organizational activities, rules, and behavior that can be seen and observed;

- **Culture** — the collection of values and norms that differentiate one group from another;

- **Values** — the stated principles on which the organization functions;

- **Norms** — the accepted, traditional, expected, and reinforced standards or behaviors in a given culture.

If we accept the definition of **ethics** as *the principles of conduct governing an individual or a group,* then we can see that **ethical culture in an organization** is *the collection of principles regarding right and wrong in certain groups.* Articulating values and transforming them into norms is the goal of all culture-change efforts.

It is easy to see how a conflict between organizational culture and ethical guidelines initiated by management will result in a win for the culture and failure for the change initiative. The unwritten rules and norms of an organization are far more powerful than concepts and ideas. Thus, if an organization is committed to an ethical approach, it must understand culture and how to change it.

Two American pioneers in this field, Hay and Gray, have done a review of various approaches to business ethics. They contend that ethical orientation can be categorized into three styles: profit maximization, trusteeship, and quality of life.[1]

In the "profit maximization" style, management operates out of raw self-interest and is constrained only by legal limits. Money and wealth are the driving values, with people seen as commodities to be bought and sold. On our Ethical Leadership Scale, this orientation would be classified as either compliance with the law (2.0) or staying out of trouble (1.0). Basically, the organization focuses on employees, customers, and community only when mandated. Conditions

ETHICAL LEADERSHIP SCALE—BASIC
5.0 Ethical Exemplar
4.0 Ethical Culture
3.0 Ethical Leadership
2.0 Compliance with Internal and External Laws and Regulations
1.0 Ethical Minimum—Stay Out of Trouble

ripe for profits from this approach are an economy of scarcity and an abundance of labor. Given these conditions, the main goal is to produce a sufficient quantity of products to meet an existing demand. Quality is not the most important issue because, in an economy of scarcity, there is little or no competition for products or services.

In the "trusteeship" style, management sees itself as responsible for achieving an equitable balance among customers, suppliers, creditors, stockholders, and community. Money and people are the driving values, with managers recognizing that employees have more than just economic needs. On our scale, this orientation would be classified as ethical leadership (3.0) because it provides proactive programs. The primary conditions that facilitate profit from this approach are the use of skilled labor and the participation in strong markets. The main goal is to maximize technology, and quality is critical because competition is severe. The major pitfall of this ethical approach is the assumption that people who meet or exceed the company's skill requirements can always be recruited and retained. While ethical implications of actions are considered, management falls far short of creating an ethical culture. Organizations that take this approach are always treating employees, customers, and community as a means rather than an interdependent part of the success equation. When the short-term profit motive clashes with the long-term interest of employees, customers, and community, the organization usually chooses the direction that results in profit — often at a significant cost to itself in the long term.

In the "quality of life" style, leadership assumes responsibility for its ethics and its values. Enlightened self-interest, employee development, customer productivity, and community well-being become the prepotent factors in making decisions, with leaders believing that what is good for society is good for their company. Employee dignity is a predominant concern and people are considered as important as money. On our scale, this orientation would be classified as ethical culture (4.0), and would probably result in the organization becoming an ethical exemplar (5.0). The primary conditions that facilitate profits from this approach are empowered people, interdependence, and trust. Given these conditions, the main goals are to maximize organizational, human, and information capital and to use financial capital as a catalyst for future growth. As long as we operate in a free society in which truth is valued and trust is achieved, this style will not only result in the greatest public good, but also generate the greatest amount of wealth for buying our goods and services and perpetuating the cycle. Leaders who create this type of culture will strengthen the connection between ethics and profits.

Table 2 provides us with a quick summary of the above discussion.

In conclusion, taking a cultural approach to ethics means creating the vision, values, and norms that support the connection between profits and ethics. This chapter will explore these three ingredients of culture and a process for change.

TABLE 2. The Three Ethical Orientations

	Profit Maximization	Trusteeship	Quality of Life
Management Style	Raw self-interest; constrained only by legal limits	Commitment to equitable balance	Responsibility for ethics and values
Driving Values	Money and wealth	Money and people	Enlightened self-interest, employee development, customer productivity, community well-being
Perception of People	Commodities to be bought and sold	Employees seen as whole persons with unique needs	Employee dignity is a predominant concern

OVERVIEW

Vision

Creating an ethical culture means empowering people to do the right thing for the company, the customer, and the community.

Assumptions

These are the assumptions related to the connection between profits and an ethical culture. In an ethical culture, the environment does all the following:

- Supports the development of organizational, human, and information capital;

- Ensures that all relationships are conducted honestly;

- Creates a sense of pride, purpose, and persistence in the organization's goals;

- Increases customers' trust, confidence, and comfort in doing business with the organization;

- Reduces the need for security measures to deal with fraud, theft, and other illegal practices within the organization.

Principles

1. Creating an ethical culture must begin with a vision that includes employees, customers, and communities.

2. An ethical culture must be guided by values that anchor the vision.

3. An ethical culture must be supported by norms and policies that influence desired behaviors in the organizational environment.

Rating Scale for Culture

This scale will help you see where you are and where you want to be.

5.0 Congruence between stated values and operating procedures

4.0 Transference of values to employees, customers, and communities

3.0 Behavior change supported and modeled by senior management

2.0 Motivational programs to rally support for the vision, values, and norms

1.0 Awareness of stated values

THE ISSUES

The Need for Vision

Creating an ethical culture begins with a vision of the organization and its relationship to the world. This vision is rooted in how we view the organization and that relationship, and represents how inclusive we are. A meaningful and believable vision can go a long way toward mobilizing employee enthusiasm. If employees come to believe their organization has a real sense of purpose, then their pride and perspective improve. Conversely, if they come to believe the company is motivated only by profit, then their commitment, loyalty, and trust diminish. After all, if the company deceives its customers, why would employees believe that it wouldn't deceive them as well?

Over the past 20 years, two major forces have had a significant relevance for organizational ethics:

1. An emphasis on short-term profits and quarterly results, which tends to narrow the ethical vision of organizations;

2. A growing sophistication among customers and new demands for elevated relationships. Customers are now seeking trusted advisors and avoiding vendors who are only pushing a product.

Unfortunately, the first force has been the stronger, giving us rampant indications of a narrow vision. Since boards of directors have been under enormous pressure to satisfy shareholders on a quarterly basis, many investments that may have had great potential for long-term return have been abandoned, postponed, or set aside. Sadly, a good share of those programs could be considered ethical in nature. As a result, many companies have become more reactionary in their "operating" vision.

This lack of vision has manifested itself in several disturbing internal problems. Corporate cultures driven without regard for people or relationships cause a great deal of individual stress and loss of productivity. The stress generated by negative norms and inappropriate management behaviors can affect people in three distinct ways. First, it may cause direct physical problems such as hypertension, ulcers, and cardiovascular disease. Second, it may adversely influence behavior, leading or contributing to smoking, overeating, high alcohol consumption, accidents, and similar dangers. Third, it may cause overreactions to physical symptoms, prompting illness behaviors such as staying home from work and avoiding healthy activity.[2]

It is important to realize that modifiable risk factors that contribute to positive health behaviors and organizational health include the norms, values, and practices of the workplace and management, as well as personal factors such as lack of knowledge, skills, and motivation. For example, consider the impact . . .

— *on a person's productivity* when an organization is rigid and autocratic, when it is unclear where a person fits into an organization, or when roles and responsibilities are ambiguous;

— *on organizational productivity* when management does not make use of employees' talents and resources (conversely, think of the energy generated when people are able to maximize their talents);

— *on a person's health* when business strategy revolves entirely around profit, with little consideration for quality, service, people, or ethics;

— *on organizational health* when promotions are based more on personal contacts than on team contributions or witheld because there is systematic bias against certain groups of people; when pay and status are not tied to performance; or when recognition comes only when an employee does something wrong;

— *on a person's productivity* when insufficient training is provided to do the job, when managers don't know how to run effective meetings, or when creativity is stifled;

— *on organizational productivity* when plans are not communicated, when more effort is required to support bureaucracy than to get the "real job" done, or when it is difficult to get the information you need to do your job;

— *on people's health* when the values of the business are totally out of alignment with the values of employees or when the organization is perceived to perform no socially useful purpose.[3]

Lack of vision is not limited to the corporate world. For example, drug abuse is a bane of urban life and beyond. Poverty and homelessness are increasing, and the gap between the rich and poor has become more painfully obvious. Over 40 million people in the United States are without health insurance, and the educational system is producing more functional illiterates than it ever has in the past. Organizations cannot divorce themselves from these issues or delude themselves that they are somehow immune. There are holes in the boat. Lounging in the captain's chambers will not secure survival.

Fortunately, some companies *are* capitalizing on ethical opportunities:

- They believe that human capital is a potent source of economic gain; therefore, they are investing in the growth and retention of their valuable resources.

- They believe that when the customer wins, they win; therefore, they are establishing interdependent relationships that result in mutual productivity and profitability gains.

- They believe that the earth one day will be one community—the only community. Therefore, they are looking for ways to safeguard and enhance the environment, not to exploit it.

Such beliefs, and the inclusive view that shapes them, are typically encapsulated in the vision statements of those companies. In this regard, leaders need to check the inclusivity of their own corporate vision statements by assessing the extent to which employees, customers, and the community are represented. Specifically, they need to ensure that the vision statement (1) represents the interdependent relationship between the company and its stakeholders, and (2) reflects a belief that the company wins when employees, customers, and community win. Here are two simple examples:

- *"We win when the customer wins."*

- *"We maximize our profits by maximizing customer profits."*

The Role of Values

To understand the "ethical edge," we must see the connection between vision, values, and strategy. Understanding this connection requires a fundamental view that organizations consist of a variety of stakeholders in a variety of communities.[4] The success of the organization is largely due to the choices and actions of all stakeholders in their respective communities. It is axiomatic that corporate strategy must reflect an understanding of the values of organizational members, stakeholders, and communities and an understanding of the ethical nature of strategic choice.

Few organizations have articulated a well-defined set of values that serve as decision-making guidelines and anchors in a "sea of change." However, most organizations do recognize values. In a review of the codes of conduct, mission statements, and business creeds of several organizations, these values appear frequently:

Profits	Respect
Quality	Fairness
Integrity	Honesty
Commitment	Equality of opportunity
Capability	Openness
Collaboration	Empowerment
Customer Focus	Confidentiality
Compliance	Interdependence
Learning	Responsibility

Moreover, we increasingly find that organizations want to be clear about what values drive their decisions and influence their behavior. And many are learning that it is critical to articulate and communicate these values to all employees in a variety of media on a frequent basis.

The articulation of values is not free of difficulties. It is often beset by three problems in particular. These are associated respectively with individualism, organizational hierarchy, and resistant attitudes toward change.

First, many people are uncomfortable about sharing their values. They view the individual as the sole judge of what is right and what is wrong. This thinking leads to a personal and situational view of ethics, namely, "what I do is my own business." In this kind of culture, it is difficult to confront people when their values differ from those of the organization. In the book *Habits of the Heart*, Robert Bellah and his associates explore the dangers of rampant individualism in our society.[5] They suggest that if individualism is America's greatest strength, it may also be its greatest weakness if taken too far. When self-interest asserts itself at the expense of the broader community, then it becomes a problem.

Second, some organizations feel that roles determine values. For example, executives who feel it is their duty as corporate citizens to achieve profit objectives independent of the effects on employees, customers, and community satisfy one value while they violate several others. The whole notion that different levels of an organization have different moral license and privileges must be challenged.

Third, some organizations believe that people's values cannot be changed and that any effort to do so is impractical. This belief leads to a "get along, go along" view of ethics. For example, many people in sales are heard to say, "It's accepted practice to provide under-the-counter payments in this business. If you don't do it, you don't sell." Confronting the justification—"in this business, everyone does it"—requires a great deal of courage, particularly in well-established subgroups, where these problems are most likely to arise. In addition, the belief that values are ingrained and cannot be changed leads to a victimized view of ethics. The bottom line is that we must articulate our values with the belief that we can and will transform these values into the norms that define our organizational culture.

The Movement to Ethical Norms

The major challenge of ethically shaping the environment is to transform our stated values into the norms that drive organizational behavior. Only in this way can we actually change the organizational culture.

Clearly, such an effort requires a systematic process of change. To fulfill that requirement effectively, we may adopt the **5D process**—design, diagnosis, development, delivery, and determination. Here we shall take a closer look at the stages of 5D and what they involve.

THE 5D PROCESS

Design. Every organization has strengths and weaknesses relative to its articulated values; therefore, a culture-change effort must begin with a clear statement of the desired end-state: what we want the culture to look and feel like.

Diagnosis. An accurate diagnosis assesses employee perceptions of the current values and norms within the organization. For this purpose, two methods are highly useful:

- Meeting formally and informally with employees at every organizational level;

- Gathering data through surveys.

In this way, we can see where a company stands in relation to its stated values. Top management's level of commitment to those values must be unconditional if the culture-change effort is to succeed. That commitment includes support for a full articulation of values—many culture-change efforts fail because articulating values becomes little more than an empty exercise in making proclamations.

Some companies use a bottoms-up approach in articulating values, while other companies use a top-down approach. Independent of the approach, it is critical to learn three things:

- Employees' perceptions of how important the values are to them;

- Whether the values are really institutionalized in the organization;

- Whether adherence to the values is getting better or worse.

The result of the diagnosis is a comprehensive understanding of which values are strong or weak in the existing culture. In addition, the diagnosis should provide information on the perceived commitment and capacity of the organization to transform weak norms into strong ones.

Development. Effective and lasting change requires a broad base of leadership skills and support within the organization. Developing skills and support usually involves a multifaceted approach to change. Typically, development includes four activities:

1. *Communication.* This involves sharing the results of the organizational diagnosis and explaining the effect of culture on organizational behavior, personal performance, and business objectives.

2. *Involvement.* Here we ensure that activities aimed at increasing commitment and enhancing capacity occur with the participation of people from all appropriate levels. Often, involvement takes the form of cross-functional task forces and teams.

3. *Skill Enhancement.* Usually we are required to improve the leadership skills, relating skills, thinking skills, and change-agent skills of key players in the organization who will lead the change effort.

4. *Planning.* Setting specific goals and time lines for changing the organizational norms is a definite requirement. Planning means deciding how the changes and goals will be implemented. In some cases, that might mean continuing specific task forces, modifying the organizational structure, or giving additional responsibilities to existing functions.

Delivery. Many culture-change efforts fail because they treat diagnosis or development as the goal line and neglect delivery. It is a highly important stage and, for most organizations, perhaps the most difficult part of any change effort. Delivery includes those activities specifically aimed at increasing commitment, enhancing capacity, and mobilizing support from leaders and employees.

The principles of effective delivery include:

- Leadership role modeling;
- Rewards and recognition for desired behavior;
- Ongoing discussion of the vision, values, and goals for the change effort;
- Feedback on results achievement.

Leadership-modeling behavior sets the tone for the culture. People take their cues from their leaders, whether those cues are implicit or explicit. If a leader encourages the sale of a product that a customer does not need, then employees will follow that example. If leaders remain silent when codes of conduct are broken, then these guidelines will not be taken seriously.

Reward systems must be designed to reinforce desired behaviors in the culture. There are very few cultures in which managers are called into the executive suite to be applauded for their ethics (think of the last time you heard of any company president calling a special meeting to recognize a manager for supporting personal growth).

For ethics to be taken seriously, leaders need to recognize exemplary ethical behavior as well as revenue-generating proficiency. Recognition should not be limited to one individual. The reward system should provide opportunities for peers to recognize the extent to which employees adhere to desired cultural norms. This can be done through multiple-rater assessments that provide opportunities for peers to give confidential feedback on behaviors that support core values. And unless ethical behaviors are included in performance reviews, they will not be considered as important as other behaviors that may result in short-term profits but long-term disaster.

Communication must be ongoing. In his book *Thriving on Chaos*, Tom Peters implores leaders to become the vision's foremost itinerant preacher. Peters suggests, "Do not let a single day pass without taking at least two or three opportunities to deliver your three-minute stump speech on the vision and to showcase events and people (small events and front-line people) that are illustrative of initiatives which support the vision."[6] Desired norms need to be constantly recognized and reinforced through a variety of communication vehicles.

Determination. This is the final phase of the 5D process and represents a return, or cycling, to the design and diagnostic phases. Effective change is an ongoing cycle of exploration, understanding, and action: exploration of where we are leads to an understanding of where we need to go, and acting on the understanding gets us to the goal line. The important features of determination are that it builds on what has been accomplished and continues the change process.

The most critical part of the determination phase is to provide feedback on the results of the change effort. Feedback can be both individual and organizational. Individual feedback means letting colleagues know how their behaviors are affecting progress. This feedback should be concrete, behavioral, and non-judgmental. Unless individuals know how their behavior is impacting others, they do not have a choice to change that behavior. Organizational feedback means reporting on progress against objectives to the employee population. This feedback should be honest and accurate and reflect both positive and negative results. To achieve credibility, organizational feedback must acknowledge negatives, provide a balanced perspective, and inspire the commitment required to continue.

NORMS AND THE CHANGE EFFORT

Essentially, constructive corporate cultural change means creating positive norms that influence ethical behavior. These norms can best be understood in terms of "around here-isms." For instance, in an ethical culture, a norm might be

"Around here, we don't accept gifts from vendors," or "Around here, we don't use inside information to our own advantage."

In many instances of unethical behavior, it is easy to attribute all the blame to general greed or deficiencies in the individual character, but rarely is that the whole story. For instance, what were the norms in those organizations that encouraged, permitted, accepted, rewarded, or tolerated unethical behaviors? How much of the problem was cultural and how much was individual? Clearly, individuals must assume responsibility for their own behavior and be held accountable. But organizations must also ask hard questions about the environment in which individuals work if they are going to be successful in shaping the kind of environment they want.

According to David Grier, vice-president at the Royal Bank of Canada, "There is a fundamental difference between developing an ethical corporate policy . . . and making sure that employees don't lie, steal, cheat, discriminate, engage in sexual harassment, etc." He goes on to say:

> Many business people haven't thought this difference through and many corporate codes of ethics don't seem to reflect this difference. Many talk a lot about what is required of employees, without saying very much about the conduct and obligations the corporation requires of itself.
>
> From the ethical perspective, the foundation has to be shared values. If the value system of a company is not tended and is not continually re-expressed and renewed, and it is not backed up by strategies, structures, and systems designed to bring it into actual practice, then it will become mere lipservice.
>
> It is persistent effort to ensure consistent application of the values in the development of strategy, structure, and systems, and a solid coherence between them that is most likely to secure the commitment of staff. In other words, a positive ethical perspective has to be built into the whole warp and woof of business management.[7]

Once again, I believe that the corporate culture defines the ways in which an organization treats its employees, its customers, and its community. In an ethical culture, people are assisted in obtaining fulfillment in their jobs; customers are seen as interdependent partners; and the community is viewed as a resource to be enhanced.

Unfortunately, realigning corporate culture is not an easy task. Even with a strong commitment and an effective process such as 5D, successful culture change takes anywhere from three to five years. Yet my experience clearly demonstrates that a commitment to create an ethical culture positively impacts the organization, even in the earliest stages of the change effort.

EXEMPLAR

In the area of corporate culture, we may easily find an exemplar in Levi Strauss and Company of San Francisco. Levi Strauss is a well-known leader in corporate philanthropy. It is distinguished by its unusual effort to get employees to take ownership of charitable contributions by having them decide where a large portion of the philanthropic budget goes. It also became the first multinational company to develop a code of conduct designed to ensure that workers making their products anywhere in the world are safe and treated with dignity and respect.

At the Levi Strauss Web site, this exemplar directly states its ethical stance as follows:

> Our values are fundamental to our success. They are the foundation of our company, define who we are, and set us apart from the competition. They underlie our vision of the future, our business strategies, and our decisions, actions, and behaviors. We live by them. They endure. The four core values are at the heart of Levi Strauss & Co.: Empathy, Originality, Integrity, and Courage. These four values are linked. As we look at our history, we see a story of how our core values work together and are the source of our success.

Levi Strauss is a company that attributes its success to its adherence to core values. This is a perfect example of how ethics and profits are not exclusive of each other, but actually go hand in hand. Indeed, ethical imperative and economic imperative are synergistic, not competitive. I highly recommend that you visit the Web site—at www.levistrauss.com—and read the further description of vision and values there.

THE CHALLENGE

Creating an ethical culture means empowering people through investments in human and information capital and instilling employees with a passion for integrity. As such, culture change is the critical factor in ethical enhancement. If an organization creates and sustains an ethical culture, then the way it deals with people, customers, and communities is fairly automatic. The ethical organization simply does the right thing.

As we have seen, the key principles for achieving an ethical culture center on:

- Creating an ideal vision of the ethical organization;
- Defining the values that anchor that vision;
- Shaping an environment that transforms the values into norms so that the ideal can eventually be achieved.

That ideal is, once again, to empower people to do the right thing for the company, the customer, and the community.

The challenge for ethical leaders is to ask the hard questions before they act. In today's fast-paced and fast-changing business world, where time is seen as a competitive weapon, executives are vulnerable to leaving the hard questions unanswered. In order to create an ethical culture, leaders must invest their time in the vision, values, and norms that give people a sense of pride in their organizations and that empower them to do the right thing.

REFERENCES

1. Hay, R., and Gray, E. "Social Responsibilities of Business Managers." *Academy of Management Journal,* March, 1977.
2. Sloan, R. *Investing in Employee Health.* San Francisco: Jossey-Bass, 1987.
3. Bellingham, R., and Cohen, B. *Managing for Health and Productivity.* Kelly Communications, 1987.
4. Freeman, E. R., and Gilbert, D. R. *Corporate Strategy and the Search for Ethics.* Englewood Cliffs, New Jersey: Prentice Hall, 1988.
5. Bellah, R., Sullivan, W., and Tipton, S. *Habits of the Heart.* San Francisco: University of California Press, 1985.
6. Peters, T. *Thriving on Chaos.* New York: Knopf, 1987.
7. Grier, D. *Globe and Mail,* December 13, 1989, p. B2.

2

Winning through People

INTRODUCTION

It is very common in organizations to hear leaders talk about people as the most valuable and valued asset, but it is very uncommon to see a consistent set of actions and initiatives that support that talk. In most organizations, the notion of people as value — or human capital — goes no further than empty slogans that cause more cynicism than satisfaction.

Dealing ethically with people means more than having a fair compensation system. It involves consideration of a person's physical, emotional, intellectual, and spiritual needs. Physically, those needs might include compensation, safe and healthy working conditions, and a pleasant environment. Emotionally, those needs might include respect, involvement, teamwork, and consideration for family issues. Intellectually, those needs might include opportunities for growth, training, variety, and support for personal development. And spiritually, those needs might include a sense of community, connectedness, and purpose.

An ethical organization is driven to treat its employees as ends and not merely as a means for generating profits. An ethical organization understands the principle of human capital. Its leaders know that by developing human resources, they will increase the value of those resources. They strengthen the connection between profits and the development of people, thus achieving ethical goals as well as traditional business objectives.

OVERVIEW

Vision

Winning through People *means treating employees as whole persons with unique values, differences, and needs.*

Assumptions

These are the assumptions related to the connection between profits and treating people right. When employees are treated right, we see these results:

- People are considered as more than "pairs of hands."

- Recruitment and retention efforts are enhanced.

- Productivity and morale are improved.

- More constructive, interdependent relationships are formed.

- Quality, innovation, and teamwork all improve.

Principles

Winning through People requires a multifaceted approach that includes:

1. *Developing* employees in ways that increase their productivity and value.

2. *Promoting* health and safety.

3. *Supporting* a sense of balance in employees' lives.

4. *Valuing* differences.

Rating Scale for Winning through People

The following scale will help you to assess where you are and to set goals for the people-oriented dimension of your business.

5.0 Movement to an exemplar for winning through people

4.0 Creation of a culture that nurtures personal and professional growth through innovative performance management, developmental opportunities, succession planning, and the like

3.0 Provision of proactive people programs such as day care, employee assistance, and health promotion

2.0 Compliance with the law by observing Equal Employment Opportunity (EEO) requirements

1.0 Avoidance of trouble with people, such as avoidance of labor-relations problems.

THE ISSUES

Employee Development

The ethical challenge for companies is to create an educational core of generic skills for all employees. The ethical advantage requires the creation of psychological contracts with employees in which employers empower workers with skills that increase their street value. The old contract with employees revolved around the exchange of job security for company loyalty. The new contract is built on the agreement that the company will provide developmental opportunities in exchange for associate commitment for the duration of the relationship.

The ethical advantage also requires employee contributions to the organization in the form of improved functional applications that will increase the company's competitive advantage. Since a large share of economic productivity growth is a result of the synergistic interaction of human and information capital,[1,2] it makes sense to invest in people and their ideas. In short, the investment in education is sound from an ethical as well as economic perspective. Of all areas, education yields the best return on investment as long as it is done well; this is also the area that causes the most problems when done poorly or not done at all.

It is generally agreed that the United States faces a triple-deficit threat: the trade deficit, the budget deficit, and the education deficit. While the first two are frightening, the third could be disastrous. By the time U.S. students graduate from high school, they rank thirteenth among the top 14 industrialized nations in math scores.[3] If this situation continues and we remain near last place among the "informationalized" countries, the competitive position of American industry will be jeopardized.

Complicating this matter on the business front is the fear that development investments will backfire—that people will learn skills and then leave, lured by competitors who can afford higher salaries for the educated precisely because they do not invest in people development. What companies with this fear fail to realize is that in offering development and thus empowering people, organizations create the image of a desired employer. And those organizations will actually *attract* the best talent as values shift and "making a life" becomes as important as "making a living." It is also unlikely that the best educated members of the workforce will gravitate toward companies who do not invest in people, because they are smart enough to realize that short-term gain may translate into long-term stagnation. In the end, the lack of people development is what will backfire as more enlightened companies pull ahead with their increasingly skilled and highly loyal employees. Investing in employee development is an ethical initiative that results in economic benefits.

Health and Safety

The effect of work on an employee's health and well-being is an ethical issue of major proportions. While most organizations see health as a tool for preventing losses as well as a responsibility, few see it as a vehicle for enhancing individual productivity and organizational health.

Some progressive companies, however, have realized significant returns on investment from their health-promotion efforts. Johnson & Johnson and AT&T both report at least a two-dollar return for every dollar invested in comprehensive health-enhancement programs.[4,5,6] In making significant investments, these companies were motivated by two things: their belief that health promotion would contribute to the human capital of the firm, and indications that this would be the best strategy for containing health-care costs.

As most executives know, health-care costs are rising astronomically. In the United States, the total health-care bill exceeded one trillion dollars in 2000, more than 15 percent of the Gross National Product (GNP). Employers paid almost 30 percent of that cost in direct health-care expenses. Those costs can be translated into direct effects on the bottom line. And these costs are rising at 15 to 20 percent per year—a rate of increase almost four times that of the Consumer Price Index.[7] If this rate continues, health-care costs will soon overtake corporate profits altogether.

If those figures are not enough, the Prudential Insurance Company of New York has determined that it costs $500,000 to recruit and retrain a replacement for a high-level executive who dies from a heart attack at age 50. In addition, an estimated 60 to 70 percent of all employee insurance claims arise from such problems as smoking, obesity, and alcoholism.[8] Indeed, more than 50 percent of all illnesses are lifestyle related, which means that they can be prevented.[9] And these are just the economic costs. The human costs may be even more significant.

Safety is also an ethical issue, as the way an organization treats safety demonstrates how committed it is to fundamental human considerations and employee rights. Like the cost of quality, there is definitely a cost associated with the effectiveness of accident-prevention efforts. Most companies do not have a system that identifies the magnitude of this cost; thus, they have difficulty with attempts to prioritize safety needs against other demands on limited resources.

The consequences of accidental events can be segregated into two major categories: human and economic. While the human category is of major concern, one must also look at the economic aspects to ensure proper allocation of resources. Examples of costs that fall into the economic category are workers compensation, property damage, wage subsidies to injured workers, overtime costs, increased supervisory time, lost efficiency, production downtime, extra hiring costs, and training costs.

Leaders who are genuinely interested in winning the right way recognize the fundamental importance of health and safety. The building blocks for organizational development are analogous to Abraham Maslow's hierarchy for individual development. Just as food and shelter must be secured before a person has a reasonable chance to aspire toward a feeling of belonging, self-esteem, and self-actualization, health and safety issues must be addressed before an organization can aspire to higher levels of organizational development. For ethical reasons as well as business reasons, enlightened leaders promote the health and safety of their employees.

Supporting Balance

Employees are more and more determined to pursue interests that go beyond the job. And employers are recognizing that multidimensional people add value to their business. It thus makes sense, from a human and economic point of view, to support balance in people's lives.

The Conference Board of Canada surveyed 385 companies with a total of approximately 1.1 million employees and found that demographic, social, and economic changes are leading employers to reassess policies aimed at recruiting and retaining employees. The Board discovered that companies are responding to personal and family needs in a variety of innovative ways. Most common is offering more-flexible work schedules. Nearly 30 percent offer part-time work with prorated benefits, more than 25 percent offer compressed weeks, almost 20 percent offer job sharing, and several companies offer specific support for employees with children.[10] Companies are beginning to build into their value systems the understanding that they "share" the responsibility for the employees' emotional as well as economic well-being. For example, Johnson & Johnson has embarked on a proactive program that makes an employee's personal concerns a matter of corporate concern by allowing management to give employees time off (with pay) to address short-term stress-inducing problems such as child care, elder care, and family substance abuse.

As the workplace and workforce continue to change, it is likely that a new set of values will emerge and that the relative importance of certain values will shift. If current trends continue, employees will increasingly desire to attend to family needs and personal-development goals. The danger is that they may find themselves torn between family and personal concerns and demands in the workplace—a situation that would threaten workplace productivity. Ethical leaders will respond to these changes by supporting balance in employees' lives, which will go far to ensure that everyone's needs are met.

Balance also means providing equal opportunity for everyone. Among the most frequent complaints of women and minorities working their way up the corporate ladder is that they are channeled into staff rather than line positions. Staff positions typically are not on a career track leading to the office of the chief executive.

According to Catalyst, a New York–based organization that focuses on career and family issues for women, there were only 46 women serving on boards of directors of the *Fortune* 1350 in 1969 (3 percent of those serving). By 1985, the number had grown to 339 serving on 407 boards of the *Fortune* 1000 (41 percent), and by 1986, the number had risen to 395 women on 439 boards (44 percent). A substantially lower percentage of companies reported women in top management positions. Even IBM, which has a solid reputation for ensuring equal opportunity for women and blacks, did not promote its first woman to the vice-presidential level until 1985.[11]

Surveys show that when business firms came under pressure in the 1960s to expand corporate governance to include greater numbers of women and minorities, many added a women director to the board, resulting in an observable increase in the number of companies with at least one female director.[12]

As Third World and Eastern European markets continue to open, radical changes will be forced on companies competing in global markets. The closed, male-dominated system will have to adapt for its own survival, and women and minorities will have to be included in the creative efforts needed for companies to achieve global preeminence. These groups will be demanding that their values and approaches to the marketplace receive recognition and credence.

EXEMPLAR

Delta Airlines has established a unique relationship with its employees. Just *how* unique was demonstrated by the employees themselves when, as a token of their appreciation for Delta's commitment to people, they pooled their resources and bought a Boeing 727 airplane for the company. This type of relationship is extraordinary, especially given the absence of loyalty in so many corporations.

Delta expresses its vision as "connecting youth to the world" and further explains:

> Our values are fundamental to our success. They are the foundation of our company, define who we are, and set us apart from the competition. They underlie our vision of the future, our business strategies, and our decisions, actions and behaviors. We live by them. They endure.

In putting those values into practice, Delta does all the following:

- Funds programs that promote the health and well-being of youth;

- Aims to ensure a healthy start in life by supporting organizations that address some of society's most formidable youth and childhood diseases;

- Supports programs that help young people develop strong character, leadership skills, and positive self-esteem, as well as programs teaching personal development, conflict resolution, and team building;

- Promotes organizations and programs that help young people embrace differences and that enrich an understanding of diverse peoples and cultures;

- Supports developing-country initiatives, diversity education, and cultural arts.

To accomplish its mission, Delta commits over $16 million annually to four Signature Partners and other worthy organizations. Delta also supports and promotes employee volunteer efforts through its Community Partners program. With its contributions of time, talent, and funding, Delta contributes to the well-being of the more than 300 communities it serves. It strives to provide a hands-on approach, recognizing every day that sometimes it takes more than an airplane to help lift someone off the ground.

THE CHALLENGE

The main point of this chapter is that winning through people means treating individuals as whole persons with unique physical, emotional, intellectual, and spiritual needs, values, and differences. Ethical leadership revolves around four key principles: developing employees, promoting health and safety, supporting balance, and valuing differences.

The first challenge of the ethical executive is to confront deficiencies in each of those fundamental areas and to fix them. Beyond that, the ethical leader has four major goals:

- To inspire people through the vision and values;

- To empower people with skills and support;

- To build teamwork through cross-functional interdependence;

- To free people to initiate through responsibility and authority.

Meeting these difficult challenges requires tremendous dedication, but it will clearly communicate to employees that they are the organization's key resources.

REFERENCES

1. Carkhuff, R. R. *The New Age of Capitalism.* Amherst, Massachusetts: HRD Press, 1988.
2. Carkhuff, R. R. *Empowering the Creative Leader.* Amherst, Massachusetts: HRD Press, 1989.
3. Dertouzos, M., Lester, R. and Solow, R. *The MIT Commission on Industrial Productivity: Made in America.* Cambridge, Massachusetts: MIT Press, 1989.
4. Bellingham, R., Johnson, D., McCauley, M., and Mendes, A. "Projected Cost Savings from AT&T Communications Total Life Concept (TLC) Process," in chapter 3, *Health Promotion Evaluation,* J. Opatz, ed. Stevens Points, Wisconsin: National Wellness Institute, 1987.
5. Anderson, D., and Jose, W. "Employee Lifestyle and the Bottom Line: Results from the Stay Well Evaluation." *Fitness in Business,* October, 1987.
6. Bly, J., Jones, R., and Richardson, J. "Impact of Worksite Health Promotion on Health Care Costs and Utilization: Evaluation of Johnson and Johnson's Live for Life Program." *Journal of American Medical Association,* 256(23), December 19, 1986.
7. Health Care Finance Administration, 1988.
8. Blue Cross Blue Shield of Maryland, 1989.
9. Centers for Disease Control, Atlanta, Georgia, 1967.
10. Gibb-Clark, M. "Firms Meeting Family Needs." *The Globe and Mail,* July 13, 1989.
11. Council on Economic Priorities, *Rating America's Corporate Conscience.* 1987, p. 23.
12. Kesner, I. "Director's Characteristics and Committee Membership: An Investigation of Type, Occupation, Tenure, and Gender." *Academy of Management Journal,* vol. 31, 1988.

3

Winning with Customers

INTRODUCTION

Customers demand more from their suppliers than ever before. They demand the highest-quality products, services, and solutions at the lowest possible price; products and solutions customized to meet their unique needs; products and services delivered as required just in time all the time; and excellent, immediate service when problems or concerns arise. In the age of abundance, we expect these demands from our customers. They are a given. If we don't meet the demands, a competitor will.

But a new set of expectations is emerging from customers, expectations that many companies may not be prepared to meet. These new expectations revolve around customer demand for integrity, interdependence, and growth. Customers are disgusted by manipulation and impatient with surveys probing their satisfaction. And often they are suspicious about who benefits in "partnership" and "immersion" relationships.

Dealing ethically with customers is one of the best strategies for responding to the new set of customer expectations. The rub is that ethics, by definition, cannot be a clever, new manipulation game. It has to be real. This chapter explores the ingredients for customer success in the area of integrity.

OVERVIEW

Vision

Winning with Customers *means conducting all interactions with the highest levels of integrity and interdependence.*

Assumptions

These are the assumptions that strengthen the connection between profits and customer ethics. When companies treat customers right, we see these results:

- Interdependent relationships in which both parties realize productivity and profitability gains;

- The organization as a preferred provider in a customer world increasingly concerned with ethics;

- Improved employee pride in the organization;

- Heightened importance of ethics in all transactions.

Principles

Winning with customers is a multidimensional approach that must incorporate these practices:

1. Thinking about customer benefits before product development;

2. Ensuring customer safety when producing/manufacturing products;

3. Relating constructively and honestly with customers while marketing the product;

4. Insisting on fairness toward customers when distributing and servicing the product.

Rating Scale for Winning with Customers

This scale will help you determine where you are and where you want to be.

5.0 Interdependent, "grow-grow" relationships with customers

4.0 Immersion in the customer's business as a "partner"

3.0 An obsession with customer benefits and win-win relationships

2.0 A passion for customer satisfaction

1.0 An orientation toward customer manipulation

THE ISSUES

Product Development

The creation of the atomic bomb is a dramatic example of how ethical issues are important in the early stages of any product-development activity. Now, of course, with new advances in DNA research and biogenetic engineering, ethical issues are constantly arising. As these issues multiply, many institutes are being established to provide research and guidance. For example, the Stanford Center for Biomedical Ethics (SCBE) engages in interdisciplinary research on moral questions arising from the complex relationships among medicine, science, and society. The products of the typical organization may not prompt such a reaction, but this does not liberate them from the need for ethical consideration.

Most companies run into ethical issues to some degree in terms of their products. How they resolve those issues, or whether they even acknowledge them, is another thing altogether. For example, more than a thousand people die every day in the United States as a result of smoking cigarettes,[1] yet tobacco companies still hire consultants to help them find creative ways to hook adolescents on smoking. What ethical conflicts does this present for the employees of those companies, or for the consultants? Consider, too, the production of increasingly realistic software for interactive games involving violence and sexual abuse. What effect will it have on our children to be exposed to "reality" games that desensitize the user to killing, rape, and abuse? Many people regard this as one of the most pressing ethical issues we now face. Yet do the companies that produce the software? And again, what ethical conflicts does this present for company employees?

In the twenty-first century, organizations will find it increasingly necessary to deal with the ethical ramifications of their products. More and more prospective employees will themselves demand it, wanting to know about the types of products that the company produces and the process by which it resolves the ethical issues surrounding those products.

Product Safety

Foremost among these issues is product safety, which scored an impressive comeback as a political issue in the 1960s after a period of dormancy during and following World War II.[2] The tragedies that arose from design deficiencies in the drug thalidomide and the Chevrolet Corvair (the subject of Ralph Nader's first book, *Unsafe at Any Speed*) were instrumental in reawakening public interest. Now the growing technological content, performance expectations, and potency of many products appear to have increased the risk and hazard of malfunction.[3]

Public demands in this area have become more complex and serious for corporations because of the increased degree of liability attributed to the manufacturer for the use of its products. It seems the manufacturer's legal position has been eroded by a tendency to hold the manufacturer liable for injury regardless of negligence on its part.[4] The issue here is not the wanton filing of lawsuits, but the willingness of government to legislate or courts to rule in favor of plaintiffs, thus punishing companies. Consequently, it is incumbent upon manufacturers to take into account potential liability issues at the earliest stages of product development.

In this context, four major issues heavily influence the product-development function:

- Public interest
- Quality assurance
- Ecology
- Solid waste

Each will be discussed briefly below.

Public Interest. Advocates of public interest have placed products under increasing scrutiny for performance, design standards, and product composition. This surveillance has resulted in product recalls, public warnings, and customer refunds that frequently entail considerable expense and loss of sales. For instance, automobile recalls to correct a single defect can cost tens of millions of dollars.

Quality Assurance. This has made a substantial impact on product development. Product engineers are now expected to understand the circumstances in which a product will be used and misused, anticipate the effects of aging and changing conditions on its performance, and incorporate these factors into product specifications. Product-design engineers are expected to meet performance and cost criteria while being cognizant of potential social demands. And in an increasingly technological age, executives must consider the downside potential of using technology for destructive purposes. For example, phones can now be programmed to ring busy for selected numbers. Should phone manufacturers provide the software that enables customers to prevent access from "undesirable" people?

Ecology. Concerns in this area have achieved global prominence because of the destruction of the ozone layer and worries about the greenhouse effect. The most visible example of this has been the controversy over standards for automobile emissions, originally established in the 1970 U.S. Clean Air Act amendments. These regulations could become more stringent and may result in more options for battery-powered cars in the near future.

Solid Waste. This is yet another concern affecting product development. The consumption of packaging materials amounts to millions of tons of solid waste a year in North America. Pressure to attend to this issue will increase as landfill capacity continues to shrink, litter becomes less tolerated, and resource shortages become more severe. It has already led to the development of a greater interest in using recycled materials in the manufacturing process and the redesign of products to minimize the eventual disposal difficulty.[5]

The difficulty in applying ethical standards to product development is that over time, advancements in technology may reveal potentially harmful effects that could not be anticipated. What happens when honest efforts to produce a safe product are called into question by new research? Should companies that engaged in responsible research suffer the same liabilities as companies that forged ahead with little thought?

Manufacturing

The Industrial Revolution brought about three changes that dramatically affected work methods, social relations, and moral values[6]:

- First, mechanization diminished the need for skilled craftsmen.

- Second, the increased volume of production required standardized procedures and precluded close personal interaction between owners and workers.

- Third, industrialization required people to work outside their homes and, usually, to relocate from rural communities into urban areas.

The Information Age has dramatically *reversed* all three changes.

- First, technological advances have increased the need for highly skilled labor or "knowledge workers," as management guru Peter Drucker calls them.

- Second, mass customization for adding value to specific client needs has demanded (1) high levels of information processing, which means a shift from standardized procedures to processing; and (2) constructive communication of resultant ideas with peers and supervisors, which means a shift from depersonalization to personalization.

- Third, collaborative technologies have made it possible for people to work on the same project simultaneously at a multitude of locations.

The historic background of this change merits a closer look.

The management theory that emerged from the Industrial Revolution was forwarded by American engineer Frederick Taylor in *The Principles of Scientific Management* (1911).[7] Primary among his contentions was that most workers tended to work too slowly, making any system based on a worker's initiative inefficient. Since Taylor considered human individuality cumbersome, he shaped a standardized work system that made employees replaceable, like the parts of a machine. He also divided the work process into thinking and acting — managers did the former, while workers did the latter.

Two decades later, in the 1930s, studies conducted at Western Electric[8] raised questions about Taylor's mechanistic approach to management. This body of research, known as the Hawthorne studies, suggested that worker groups had their own values, norms of behavior, and informal systems. It also demonstrated, inadvertently, that productivity increased when a work situation was constantly attended to and stimulated, regardless of the type of intervention — lights up, productivity up; lights down, productivity up again. But, more important, researchers viewed employees as members of a social system and attempted to understand how they were motivated within this context.[9] From these studies evolved a new approach to management.

Now the Information Age has emerged, demanding a further evolution in the way we think of the manufacturing process.

ETHICAL IMPACT AREAS IN MANUFACTURING

Today production managers and process engineers are beset by demands that they adopt a more inclusive definition of environmental impact in the design and operation of production processes.[10] This manufacturing problem as it relates to ethics is manifested in three ways:

- Degradation of the environment

- Health and safety in the workplace

- The quality of life of employees directly involved in the manufacturing process.

Each of those impact areas will be discussed briefly below.

Degradation of the Environment. Although environmental control requirements may not have catastrophic consequences for all companies, the impact on the production function in several industries is significant, and in some cases, regulations cannot be met with available control technology.[11] Yet on a number of fronts, significant progress has been made in overcoming the technological obstacles related to environmental protection. For example, in 1975, the steel industry had not developed a practical means of abating air pollution in the coking process, nor had electric utilities been successful in devising methods of reducing sulfur oxide emissions in ways that were technically viable and economically feasible. By 1990, however, significant progress had been made on those issues. The Environmental Protection Agency (EPA) has worked hard to make such strides more possible, taking great pains to reduce the economic dislocation likely to arise from its requirements.

Since regulations and compliance schedules generally impose deadlines, pressure is often exerted for early experimentation with new equipment. This process can be time-consuming, disruptive, and expensive. Yet unwillingness to experiment may delay the start-up of new facilities or threaten shutdowns of existing ones with the attendant loss of jobs and capacity. Ecological pressures may also dictate broader changes in raw materials, processes, and products.[12]

Health and Safety in the Workplace. The second major impact, working conditions, has received increased attention since the passage of the Occupational Safety and Health Act (OSHA) in 1970. Some of the most recent concerns relate to cumulative trauma disorders, asbestos exposure, and disabling accidents. And there is an ongoing need to attend to possible impairments to health from sustained exposure to noise, heat, dust, silica, carbon monoxide, and a host of other process-related conditions.

Quality of Life. This area seems to be experiencing the steepest upward trend in terms of its importance to workers. As we have moved from the "Tayloresque" approach to manufacturing, through the Hawthorne experiments, and into the Information Age, employees' needs and values have changed. As a result, manufacturing processes must take into account the issues that affect employee well-being.

Marketing

Many of the ethical issues facing companies today are related not to the product itself, but to the manner in which it is marketed and serviced. These issues can be categorized as follows:

- Advertising and packaging

- The selling practices of vendors

- Product and performance warranties

Each will be discussed briefly below.

Advertising and Packaging. Just as manufacturing is subject to regulatory bodies such as the EPA and OSHA, advertising and packaging is subject to the Federal Trade Commission (FTC), which monitors these areas. Since the agency's creation in 1914, its main decree has been to prohibit "unfair methods of competition." As one might guess, deceptive advertising and packaging has been at the top of the FTC's list of abuses. As television commands such a large share of the typical consumer's day, advertising in this media receives particularly close review. Essentially, companies are prohibited from the deceptive use of research studies, unsubstantiated claims, inadequate disclosure, and deceptive television demonstration.

The Selling Practices of Vendors. These have a long history of consumer complaint. Like the proverbial snake-oil salesman, the culprits are often marginal characters who fraudulently foist their goods and services on a gullible public. The 1987 movie *Tin Men* offers a good illustration in its depiction of a shady aluminum-siding vendor.

In recent years, the boom in new get-rich schemes coupled with advances in telemarketing produced a plethora of high-pressure sales tactics. Financial advisors, with only calling cards for credentials, implored thousands of people to invest in tax-shelters, limited partnerships, and "sure-fire" stocks that in many cases turned sour, causing significant hardship, if not bankruptcy, for investors.

Product and Performance Warranties. Finally, the issue of warranties has caused perhaps the greatest amount of public distress with large corporations. Promises of service and customer satisfaction often prove difficult to fulfill when problems occur with a product. Not surprisingly, consumers become frustrated and angry when companies are unresponsive to their requests for service or redress.

Under-the-counter payments. Kickbacks. False representation. Get-rich-quick schemes. These are all symptoms of an ethical crisis in marketing. They play off consumer fear and greed, reflecting a variety of "manipulation" schemes that mark a "level-one" organization. In the Information Age, an obsession for customer satisfaction and an orientation toward customer benefits will be survival requirements. Forming interdependent relationships will be necessary for growth.

EXEMPLAR

Pharmaceutical giant Johnson & Johnson, Inc., has been winning with customers for over 50 years, backed by a credo of responsibility to customers, employees, community, and shareholders. Twenty years ago, its leadership's grounding in that credo helped to prevent what seemed certain disaster for the company after it was plunged into a nightmare scenario.

On September 30, 1982, James Burke, Johnson & Johnson CEO, heard that three people in the Chicago area had died after taking Extra-Strength Tylenol capsules. Authorities found that the country's most successful over-the-counter pain reliever had been laced with lethal doses of cyanide. Within days of the first fatality report, the death toll rose to seven—all from the Chicago area. The Tylenol murders were front-page news all over the nation.

In response, Johnson & Johnson voluntarily initiated a massive recall of 31 million bottles of Tylenol capsules. Burke flew to Washington, D.C., and met with the FDA commissioner and the FBI director to jointly work out plans to effect the recall and make it impossible for the tragedy to unleash copycat crimes. He then called a meeting of 50 Johnson & Johnson company presidents and corporate staffers and made an "unequivocal decision" to put the full resources of the company behind the recall effort.

Several teams of employees tackled the complex problem of designing solid tamper-resistant packaging quick enough to resurrect consumer confidence in Tylenol. They succeeded. Shortly thereafter, on November 4, Burke introduced and demonstrated in the nation's capital a new packaging system with triple barriers to prevent tampering. Richard Schweiker, Secretary of Health and Human Services, called the new packaging system an "armored tank."

Johnson & Johnson handled this "distribution problem" correctly. But "doing it right" in the case of this company was not an isolated event; it was a result of a corporate culture driven by ethics and a commitment to customers.[13] Today, Johnson & Johnson remains a healthy and profitable company. It proudly displays its time-honored credo at its Web site (www.jnj.com).

THE CHALLENGE

As we have seen in this chapter, the principal challenge in this ethical area is to conduct all customer-related interactions with the highest levels of integrity and honesty, from product development through servicing, so that both the company and its customers win. Organizations need to check their ethics by asking themselves these basic questions:

- Are we trying to manipulate the customer or benefit the customer?

- Are our actions congruent with the strategy of developing interdependent relationships with customers?

- Do our actions meet the highest standards of integrity and honesty?

- Is our basic marketing strategy a winner?

Ethical leaders cast themselves in a helping role with their customers. Instead of viewing customers as consumers of goods and services who can easily satisfy the provider's financial problems, such leaders view them as clients or partners seeking solutions for a wide range of needs. In this new role, the provider offers integrated solutions to the customer's human, information, organizational, and financial problems.[14] In short, the challenge is to move from being self-centered to being interdependent.

REFERENCES

1. *The Surgeon General's Report. Healthy People.* Washington, D.C.: U.S. Government Printing Office, 1982.
2. Nadel, M. *The Politics of Consumer Protection.* New York: Bobbs-Merrill, 1971.
3. Ackerman, R. *The Social Challenge to Business.* Cambridge, Massachusetts: Harvard University Press, 1975.

4. Schirmer, W. "Product Liability and Reliability: The View from the President's Office," in *Consumerism: Search for the Consumer Interest,* David Aaker and George Day, eds. New York: The Free Press, 1971.

5. Cardin, F. "A Framework for Assessing the Impact of Selected Incentives for Recycling in the Paper Industry." Unpublished thesis. Harvard Business School, Cambridge, Massachusetts, 1974.

6. Andrews, K. *Ethics in Practice.* Cambridge, Massachusetts: Harvard Business School Press, 1989.

7. Taylor, F.W. *The Principles of Scientific Management.* New York: W.W. Norton, 1967.

8. Roethlisberger, F., and Dickson, W. *Management and the Worker.* Cambridge, Massachusetts: Harvard University Press, 1939.

9. Porter, L., Lawler, E., and Hackman, J. *Behavior in Organizations.* New York: McGraw-Hill, 1975.

10. Ackerman, R. *The Social Challenge to Business.* Cambridge, Massachusetts: Harvard University Press, 1975.

11. Ibid.

12. Ibid.

13. Johnson, C. *Meeting the Ethical Challenges of Leadership.* London: Sage Publications, 2001

14. Carkhuff, R.R. *The Possibilities Organization.* Amherst, Massachusetts: HRD Press, 2000.

4

Winning for the Community

INTRODUCTION

What is the mission of an ethical leader? To promote individual and corporate prosperity independent of the long-term effects on the world community? Or to create a productive and peaceful world community that supports sustainable growth for individuals, groups, and organizations? The answer to this question will determine an organization's readiness to hear the contents of this introduction.

The material we shall consider is blunt in its presentation and frightening in its implications. It is drawn heavily from two sources: *Our Common Future*,[1] based on the work of the World Commission on Environment and Development, and a more recent book, *Who Owns the Sky? Our Common Assets and the Future of Capitalism*[2] by Peter Barnes, the co-founder of

Working Assets. The essential premise of both works is that economic growth and environmental hope are inextricably linked. In short, these authors suggest that we must do the following:

- Consider economic policies and business practices in terms of sustainable development.

- Look at new ways to meet the needs of the present without compromising the ability of future generations to meet their own needs.

- Work to meet the basic needs of all, extending to people the opportunity to satisfy their aspirations for a better life.

This view operationalizes the long-term perspective with which business leaders are constantly implored to concern themselves.

We have, in general, ignored the principles of sustainable development. Our recent history testifies to that. And even as the world awakens to its past, horrified by the innumerable atrocities it has passively accepted in its brief history, it fails to awake to the present, despite atrocities mounting to heights never before imagined. We cannot seem to realize the genocide we are perpetuating with our passive acceptance of non-sustainable development policies and actions. We cannot seem to embrace the idea of sustainable development and use it as a driving force for all our actions.

It is my hope that the material below will lead you to the conclusion that we can no longer postpone the imperative of sustainable development. All communities—in interdependent relationship across planet Earth—demand this of ethical leaders.

WHERE WE HAVE BEEN

Witness just a few examples of what has happened in recent history:

- An estimated 60 million people worldwide have died of diarrhea-related diseases due to unsafe drinking water and malnutrition. Most of the victims were children.

- A drought-triggered environmental crisis in Africa put 35 million people at risk and killed more than one million people.

- A leak from a pesticides factory in Bhopal, India killed more than two thousand people, and more than 200 thousand other people were blinded and injured.

- Liquid-gas tanks exploded in Mexico City, killing a thousand people and leaving thousands more homeless.

- The Chernobyl nuclear reactor explosion in the Soviet Union sent nuclear fallout across the world, increasing the risk of human cancers, particularly in Europe.

- Agricultural chemicals, solvents, and mercury flowed into the Rhine River during a warehouse fire in Switzerland, killing millions of fish and threatening drinking water in Germany and the Netherlands.[3]

As alarming as these examples are, they only suggest the bigger picture, and might even be overshadowed by future disasters if dramatic changes do not occur immediately.

THE CASE FOR INTERVENTION: SIX KEY FACTORS

The following review of six key factors in sustainable development makes a compelling case for drastic intervention. Together, these are the factors:

1. Poverty	**4.** Food and Water
2. Population	**5.** Energy
3. Production	**6.** Species Extinction

The review includes facts drawn from *Our Common Future* and *Who Owns the Sky?* as well as implications for the ethical leader.

1. POVERTY

Facts

Developed countries account for 26 percent of the population, but consume about . . .

- 40 percent of the food,

- 85 percent of the paper,

- 80 percent of the steel,

- 80 percent of the energy.

The last three items, of course, are as much signs of development as they are symptoms of greed.

The number of years required to bring the poverty ratio down from 50 percent to 10 percent is

- 18 to 24 years, at 3 percent increase/year in per capita GDP;

- 26 to 36 years, at 2 percent increase/year in per capita GDP; and

- 51 to 70 years, at 1 percent increase/year in per capita GDP.

Implications for the Ethical Leader: There is no sin in creating wealth. In fact, economic productivity growth is essential if we are to have a positive impact on our communities. The question is *how the wealth gets distributed.* As demonstrated above, it is critical to achieve 3 percent per capita national income growth and to pursue vigorous redistribution policies.

The requirements for such growth include free market access, lower interest rates, greater technology transfer, and larger capital flows. But perhaps more important, economic productivity growth requires an investment in human and information resources, which, interacting synergistically, will create new responses to whatever challenges continue to confront us. In short, jobs and education will generate hope for the future.

2. POPULATION

Sustainable development is tied to population and poverty. Poverty reduces people's capacity to use resources in a sustainable manner, and poverty deepens in direct proportion to population growth.

Facts
Consider these population figures:

Industrialized World
1985 — 1.2 billion   2025 — estimated 1.4 billion

Developing Countries
1985 — 3.7 billion   2025 — estimated 6.8 billion

We thus can anticipate a total world population of 8.2 billion by 2025 — a 60 percent increase over roughly three decades.[4] Also consider that between 1985 and 2000, the labor force in developing countries increased by nearly 900 million people; new jobs had to be created for 60 million people every year.[5]

Implications for the Ethical Leader: Unless new jobs are created and poverty abated, the resource base on which sustainable development depends will be further eroded. The reduction of poverty is thus a first priority for businesses that are concerned about future growth and long-term

development. Without such a reduction, people will acceler-
ate in a downward spiral, resulting in a loss of hope.

3. PRODUCTION

In order to meet the demands of a growing population and to
fuel a growth economy, goods and services need to be produced. The way the production cycle is handled, from extrac-
tion of materials to disposal of wastes, plays a major role in
sustainable development.

Facts

We now manufacture about seven times the amount of goods
we manufactured in 1950. Given expected population
growth, an additional five- to tenfold increase in world
industrial output can be anticipated by the time we reach the
8 to 10 billion population mark.[6] We have witnessed trends
toward increased efficiency. The amount of raw materials
needed for a given unit of economic output dropped
throughout the past century, except in periods of world war,
for practically all non-agricultural commodities.

There is clearly a need for regulations. We cannot neglect
standards that govern such matters as air and water pollution; waste management; occupational health and safety;
energy and resource efficiency of products or processes; and
the manufacture, marketing, use, transport, and disposal of
toxic substances.[7] With regulation, abuses occur; without regulation, abuses occur with complete abandon.

For a reminder of how vital those regulations are, we have
only to look at mainland China. Its industries, most of which
use coal in outdated furnaces and boilers, are concentrated
around 20 cities. Lung cancer mortality in those cities is four
to seven times higher than in the nation as a whole, and the
difference is largely attributable to the heavy, industry-based
air pollution.[8]

In addition, there are 60 to 80 thousand chemicals now in the market worldwide, with industrialized nations generating about 90 percent of the world's hazardous wastes.[9]

Implications for the Ethical Leader: As the quantity of products and associated wastes continues to increase and the availability of disposal options continues to decrease, product development and waste disposal issues will climb to the top of priority lists. Business leaders will be required to choose between creating environmentally friendly products and fighting legislation. In addition, ethical leaders need to raise questions about dealing with countries that blatantly ignore the effect of industries on people.

4. FOOD AND WATER

All species need food and water as a source of energy to sustain their own development. Thus, we must protect food and water sources and enhance them to meet the productivity demands of a growing world population.

Facts
The world produces more food per head today than ever before—nearly 500 kilograms per head of cereals and root crops, the primary food sources. Yet approximately one billion people are not eating enough to lead fully productive working lives.[10]

Potential production capacity could sustain 11 billion people—almost twice the world's current population—at current consumption levels. If consumption goes up, the potential capacity would feed 7.5 billion. Experts predict an ultimate world population of 10 billion. Thus, unless we reduce consumption and increase sustainable development, 2.5 billion people will lack sufficient food.[11] This does not account for increasing life expectancy and decreasing infant mortality.

Shortsighted policies are leading to the degradation of the agricultural resource base on almost every continent.

Dangerous trends include soil erosion in North America, soil acidification in Europe, and deforestation and desertification almost everywhere. The latter is particularly disturbing, with the portion of land permanently degraded to desert-like conditions growing at an annual rate of six million hectares; in addition, each year about 21 million more hectares yield no economic return because of the spread of desertification.[12] To such trends we may append the growing threat of global warming, which, within 40 to 70 years, may cause the flooding of important coastal production areas.

Certainly, some of these dangers can be traced to energy use and industrial resources; but agricultural policies emphasizing increased production at the expense of environmental considerations have also contributed greatly to this alarming situation.[13]

We run into a similar problem with chemical fertilizers and pesticides. They have played a large role in production increases since the Second World War, yet over-reliance on them has raised clear warnings. Nitrogen and phosphates runoff from the excess use of fertilizers damages water resources and local water supplies, and such damage is spreading. Using pesticides enhances productivity, but over-use threatens the health of humans and the lives of other species. Continuing, long-term exposure to chemical-fertilizer and pesticide residues in food, water, and even the air is hazardous, particularly to children.

Implications for the Ethical Leader: The challenge is to meet increased food demands while enhancing ecological integrity. Clearly, starvation anywhere in our community is morally unacceptable. It is also intolerable for economic and environmental reasons. While food-relief programs reduce immediate crises, they lead to further economic marginalization of people over time. People need to be enriched with skills as well as food. Perhaps the goal should be to provide food in classrooms or training facilities.

5. ENERGY

Energy requirements are increasing rapidly, while energy resources are being depleted. As we move into a high-energy future, sustainable energy development will require that we find better ways to meet our energy needs.

Facts

In 1980, global energy consumption was about 10 terawatts, or 10 billion kilowatts. In 1987, it was estimated that if per-capita use remained at current levels, by 2025 a global population of 8.2 billion would need about 14 terawatts. If energy consumption per capita became uniform at current industrial-country levels, by 2025 that same global population would require about 55 terawatts.[14]

ENERGY KEY		
1 kilowatt	=	1000 watts of energy
1 terawatt (TW)	=	1 billion kilowatts
1 TW year	=	1 billion tons of coal

It was also estimated that at current rates, gas supplies should last more than 200 years and coal supplies about three thousand years. In terms of pollution, gas is the cleanest, oil is the next, and coal is the worst.[15]

Although worldwide reliance on renewable energy sources has been growing by more than 10 percent per year since the late 1970s, it will be some time before they make up a substantial portion of the world's energy capacity. Renewable energy systems are still in a relatively primitive stage of development, but they offer the world potentially huge primary energy sources, sustainable in perpetuity and available in one form or another to every nation on earth. A substantial and sustained commitment to further research and development is required if their potential is to be realized.[16]

The burning of fossil fuels added to the loss of vegetation cover equals carbon dioxide (CO_2) pollution. The increase in the parts per million of CO_2 in our environment has been estimated as follows:

- In 1880: 280 parts per million

- In 1980: 340 parts per million

- By 2100: 560 parts per million (projected)

At 400 parts per million, the result could be a global warming from 1.5 to 4.5 degrees on the Celsius scale. This development, which would lead to a sea-level rise of 25 to 140 centimeters, could inundate low-lying coastal areas. By the year 2025, it is possible that we will reach 400 parts per million.[17]

The United States is the principal source of carbon dioxide in the world. According to United Nations figures, in 1985 it produced 23 percent of the total. The Soviet Union produced 19 percent, followed by China with 10 percent and Japan with 5 percent. In November of 1989, the United States joined with Japan to block agreement by 68 nations to accept strong measures for curbing the release of carbon dioxide into the atmosphere. Both nations said they would not endorse a commitment to control emission of carbon dioxide by the year 2000.

These are the major sources of carbon dioxide pollution in the United States:

- Electric Power plants   —   33 percent

- Vehicles   —   31 percent

- Industries   —   24 percent

- Other   —   12 percent

Carbon dioxide and other "greenhouse" gases released by fossil-fuel combustion also acidify the environment and, of course, cause air pollution.

Implications for the Ethical Leader: Seeking out renewable, non-polluting sources of energy is a critical issue. Our current energy sources have an impact on ethical leaders not only because they cause enormous pollution problems, but also because their long-term availability for organizations is uncertain. These leaders will therefore aggressively seek out practical alternatives.

Here ethical leadership also means realizing that failures to manage the environment and to sustain development threaten to overwhelm all countries. Environment and development are not separate challenges; they are inexorably linked. Development cannot subsist on a deteriorating environmental resource base; the environment cannot be protected when growth does not account for the costs of environmental destruction. These problems cannot be treated separately by fragmented institutions and policies. They are linked in a complex system of cause and effect.[18]

As our image of community broadens to the point where we see ourselves as truly global in operations, these factors will play a larger and larger role.

6. SPECIES EXTINCTION

Just as our image of community needs to broaden to include all the world, our notion of life needs to deepen to include all biological species. Yes, we feel embarrassed over our current practices and narrow passions. And we should: We are, in effect, extinguishing entire families of plants and animals.

Facts
With the destruction of our forests, especially the rain forests, we are rapidly killing off whole species of plants and animals. In Madagascar and Western Ecuador, there were over

200 thousand species in 1950: now, fewer than half of these remain.[19]

Implications for the Ethical Leader: These are not only ecosystem issues, but economic issues as well. For example, half of all prescription medicines have their origins in wild organisms, and sales of these medicines exceed $14 billion per year.[20]

This review of the six factors in sustainable development underscores one thing: We *must* face our responsibilities to our worldwide community, as well as to our local communities. Now, in the balance of this chapter, we shall turn to some of the fundamental attitudes and behaviors of an organization ready to accept those responsibilities and involve itself in the creation of a productive community. Our hope must be that all organizations soon ready themselves for this challenge. The prosperity and freedom of North America are at stake. It cannot be overstated: The future of the world is at risk.

OVERVIEW

Vision

Winning for the Community means taking the initiative to create productive communities that are able to sustain growth and development.

Assumptions

These are the assumptions related to the connection between sustainable development and growth in economic productivity. When companies treat communities right, they do the following:

- They create the economic base that gives future generations a fighting chance for peace and prosperity.

- They improve relationships with local, state, national, and international government and civic organizations.

- They establish an image in the community of a responsible, responsive, and environmentally sensitive contributor.

- They demonstrate to employees that the organization has a mission that goes beyond self-interest.

Principles

A company that wants to do right by its community will . . .

1. *Enhance* the environment.

2. *Contribute* generously to community resources.

3. *Encourage* participation in the community.

Rating Scale for Winning for the Community

This scale will help you determine where you are and where you want to be:

5.0 Creating a productive community

4.0 Promoting community growth

3.0 Participating in community organizations

2.0 Protecting community resources

1.0 Meeting minimal regulations

THE ISSUES

Environment

At a 1989 global summit meeting, the major industrial democracies known as the Group of Seven agreed to a communiqué calling for "decisive action" to protect the global environment. This document placed the environment, an afterthought at previous summit meetings, at the top of the agenda for the world economy. While such declarations tend to express desire and determination rather than signify real commitment to change, they can and often do lead to changes in national economic policies. In North America, several companies are also giving the environment a higher place on their internal agendas.

W. S. Woolard, chairman of E. I. DuPont de Nemours Company, makes this fundamental challenge to his organization and others like it:

> Our continued existence as a leading manufacturer requires that we excel in environmental performance and that we enjoy the non-objection — indeed, even the support — of the people and governments in the societies where we operate around the world. What's at stake is the ability of much of our present manufacturing industry to continue to serve well the growing needs of society.[21]

Woolard's statement underscores the intimate relationship between environmental ethics and future business success.

As companies expand into global markets, it becomes particularly important to address environmental issues. In April of 1988, *The Economist* reported that when West Germans were asked what worried them most, twice as many listed pollution as listed unemployment. In the same month, Britain's *Financial Times* reported that 70 percent of the population in the Netherlands were prepared to forego a higher standard of living for a cleaner country. Environmental sensitivity is no longer a peripheral issue.[22]

Three Mile Island; Bhopal; Chernobyl; Valdez; the ozone layer: these are now inscribed in our collective memory as reminders that disasters can occur when we get sloppy. As a result of these catastrophes and several other environmental warning signs, the public is demanding that organizations take responsible action to protect and enhance our environment. For example:

- Agreements with waste transporters, handlers, and disposal companies are not uniformly supervised by environmental professions, nor are they documented and tracked as defensive data against future litigation and regulatory discipline action. This leaves organizations vulnerable to guilt by association. The ethical organization will want to know how its waste is being disposed.

- Most companies do not know where all their underground storage tanks are, what is or was in them, their condition, and whether soil or ground water contamination has occurred or could soon occur. When tanks leak, the costs can be high. For example, one Canadian company spent $4,700 to clean up a $50 diesel fuel spill. Inadequate monitoring and dismantling of these tanks represents a major liability. In another company, leakage from storage drums has resulted in projected costs in excess of $5 million.[23] Obviously, stringent ethical requirements have economic implications.

Most companies lack planning and resources to ensure that their facilities meet the broadest standards of cleanliness. All real estate transactions now require environmental-damage assessments, for which companies will continue to have liability. Organizations that act irresponsibly in getting rid of environmental problems may soon be subject to tougher standards. The disclosure that toxic waste is being put into delivery trucks along with gas or oil and then brought to gas stations where consumers fill their tanks with it demonstrates how persuasive and insidious the problem has become.

One major problem is that most companies have no data management system to ensure compliance, track chemical use, and guarantee that waste production meets governmental regulations, nor are they able to respond to regulatory requests and efficiently manage environmental data. The absence of such systems makes it almost impossible for companies who want to do the right thing to do it. The companies that are determined to take the ethical approach to environmental issues are developing those systems now.

Resources

H. Brewster Atwater, chairman of General Mills, Inc., of Minneapolis, has argued:

> One of the most important duties of each citizen, whether a corporation or an individual, is to work in a multitude of ways for the betterment of society. In the long run this is a self-interested proposition, in no way inconsistent with a corporation's duties to its shareholders.

Since 1970, corporate philanthropy has grown more than twice as rapidly as that of private foundations. Corporations in the United States donated an estimated $3.45 billion in 1984, approaching the $4.36 billion given by foundations. In 2000, Bill Gates set a new standard by donating $20 billion in stock to a foundation. Also in 2000, Hewlett Packard donated $7 million to nonprofits in Silicon Valley. As part of the effort by the Reagan administration to increase corporate social giving and "public-private" partnerships, its task force on private-sector initiatives set a goal in 1981 of increasing corporate giving from an average one percent of pre-tax net earnings to two percent by 1986. Figures reported by the American Association of Fund-Raising Councils show the corporate average hovering around 1.5 percent from 1982 through 1984.[24]

The California Chamber of Commerce has been promoting the formation of "Two-Percent Clubs" around the state since 1983. Minneapolis's Dayton Hudson Corporation is a strong advocate of "five-percent" giving levels.

There is, of course, an endless array of organizations and causes that solicit corporate funds. Most organizations, however, concentrate their giving in a few key areas.[25] These are the areas, along with the percentage of companies that concentrate their giving in these areas:

- Education — 40 percent
- Health and human services — 30 percent
- Civic and community — 15 percent
- Culture and art — 10 percent
- Other — 5 percent

Productive Communities

Many organizations assume that communities will provide the human resources required to maintain a steady stream of people and ideas. This assumption, which relates to the lifeblood of the future, needs to be challenged. Companies that count on the continual provision of resources must lend a hand, helping to maintain or to revitalize the communities on whom they depend.

Communities consist of homes, schools, universities, businesses, and arts-leisure facilities and organizations. They are affected by political, social, economic, and environmental factors. While businesses cannot be expected to solve all the problems of the communities in which they reside, they need to establish interdependent relationships with all the entities so that collaborative initiatives can be launched.

EXEMPLAR

Our ethical exemplar in winning with communities is PTC, a Needham, Massachusetts–based software company with four thousand employees. PTC is the leading provider of product-development software. It is committed to better education, with a corporate giving program which backs up that commitment. Currently, one million students at four thousand schools and 1,500 colleges and universities are using PTC software to help build our future.

PTC is investing its legacy of design-engineering innovation in helping students and teachers in secondary schools and universities become more technologically literate. It recognizes that we must close the gap between our vast reliance on technology and our technological illiteracy to remain competitive in the global economy. As part of a technology-education reform movement, PTC seeks to improve critical thinking and multidimensional problem-solving skills while also inspiring and preparing a growing number of students to become engineers. Its Partnership for Innovative Learning is designing an entirely new approach to teaching students how to think and create in 3D.

The Partnership: Preparing a new generation to succeed in a technology-driven world

PTC demonstrated its mission's concern for community in the immediate wake of the September 11 attacks. It donated generously to the victim relief fund, matching the contributions of employees from all over the world. The company also established a $100,000 endowment at the University of Massachusetts for students who were directly affected by the tragedy.

PTC further demonstrates its commitment to the community by sponsoring a City Year Team in Boston.

THE CHALLENGE

Leaders must explore the readiness factors in their organizations to create more-productive communities. Three fundamental indicators suggest the extent to which an organization is truly committed to making a difference: **environmental responsibility, charitable giving,** and **community involvement.**

For organizations that have demonstrated a commitment to change, the challenge is to create the capacity for change in resident communities. Homes need to become preparatory learning centers; schools need to become thinking centers; universities need to become creativity centers; and businesses need to become productivity centers.[26] This will not and cannot happen with a wish and a prayer. It will require a substantive, systematic, and comprehensive intervention that involves all members of the community. It can be done. It must be done.

REFERENCES

1. World Commission on Environment and Development. *Our Common Future.* Oxford: Oxford University Press, 1987.
2. Barnes, P. *Who Owns the Sky? Our Common Assets and the Future of Capitalism.* Washington, D.C.: Island Press, 2001.
3.–20. Ibid.
21. Woolard, E.S. Presentation to the American Chamber of Commerce (UK), London, May 4, 1989.
22. *The Economist,* April, 1988.
23. Interview with David Tostenson, Northern Telecom, July 1989.
24. Council of Economic Priorities. *Rating America's Corporate Conscience,* 1987.
25 Ibid.
26. Carkhuff, R. R., *Nation Building.* Amherst, Massachusetts: HRD Press, 2002.

5

Action Steps and Strategies

INTRODUCTION

To take action in ethical leadership, we must first and foremost be able to recognize an ethical corporate culture when we see one. This is a vital prerequisite. Most executives see ethics through a set of "compliance-colored" glasses that limits their vision of what an ethical culture might look like. Instead of constantly searching for new possibilities in the ethics-strategy connection, they fall into an avoidance mindset: "Our ethics program is working if there are no fines and no allegations of malfeasance." It is doubtful that executives with such a limited vision and mindset will be able to recognize the potential for the competitive advantage inherent in high levels of ethics. There must be an emphasis on positive direction.

In reviewing more than 100 ethical exemplars in the corporate world, many of which I have mentioned in this book, I found 10 common ingredients that, together, suggest a key to the competitive advantage for companies with highly ethical corporate cultures. They are as follows:

THE 10 INGREDIENTS OF AN ETHICAL CULTURE

1. A tradition of strong values and ethics

2. A belief at the top in the strategic importance of integrity

3. Leadership modeling and commitment

4. Explicit statements of values and beliefs, such as codes of ethics and standards of business conduct

5. Active solicitation of support from managers and employees

6. A common view that ethics is a cultural issue

7. Procedures and systems that ensure that ethics is a central part of selection and performance management

8. Tailored education and training programs

9. Multiple upward and downward communication channels

10. Broad monitoring of ethics goals

These ingredients are translated into principles and action steps in the first section of this chapter. They should prove useful to executives who want to renew the focus on ethics in their organizations or transform their organizations from unacceptable ethics (levels 1.0 or 2.0) to acceptable ethics (level 3.0) or advantageous ethics (levels 4.0 or 5.0). The second section of this chapter focuses on strategies for accountability, which will help reinforce these principles and the goals that are selected.

PRINCIPLES AND ACTION STEPS

1. A tradition of strong values and ethics. When ethics and values are grounded in tradition, policies emerge naturally as an outgrowth of the culture.

In almost all of the ethical exemplars, major decisions in troubling times were eased by a well-defined set of values that served as anchors in gray and turbulent seas. Thus, *the first step* for the ethical executive should be to review the values that guide the organization, and to assess how accurately those values reflect how things "really work around here." It takes time and energy to develop such a tradition.

2. A belief at the top in the strategic importance of integrity. When leaders view integrity as having strategic importance, all employees begin to see the business possibilities in creating an ethical edge.

Ethical exemplars encourage other leaders to ask hard questions about issues in every phase of the business. People must feel free to disagree with, probe, challenge, and even poke fun at directions or decisions that the company is considering. One chairman suggested that executive committees should contain a jester, an ethicist, and an empiricist. The jester pokes fun at various initiatives, the ethicist raises questions of integrity, and the empiricist seeks out the facts and numbers that make for useful debate. Thus, *the second step* is (a) to ensure that all employees see the potential of sharpening the ethical edge, and (b) to create an environment that encourages people to think about and debate ethical issues as they arise or, better, to identify them before they spark a crisis.

3. Leadership modeling and commitment. When leadership demonstrates its commitment to ethics through its own behavior, employees will get the message that taking the high road will enhance their careers.

Since employees take their cues from their leaders, executive behavior has a far greater impact on employee ethics than any words, memos, or documents distributed from the executive suite. For example, participation in decision-making and corporate-values seminars lets employees know that ethics is taken seriously. And leaders benefit from this sort of participation because they have opportunities to share their thinking on case studies and receive feedback on their actions, thoughts, and feelings. Thus, *the third step* is to encourage the leadership team to demonstrate its commitment to creating an ethical edge in a variety of ways.

4. Explicit statements of values and beliefs, such as codes of ethics and standards of business conduct. When there are explicit statements of values and beliefs, employees are clear about expectations.

Clarity is essential in the definitions of desired behaviors and corporate culture. In most companies, values are vague notions or undefined lists that are supposed to guide decision making. Thus, *the fourth step* is to articulate the vision and values of the company, distribute code-of-conduct books for all employees, write standards of business conduct for all departments, and breathe life into all these documents through ongoing communications and discussions.

5. Active solicitation of support from managers and employees. When executives actively solicit the involvement and support of managers and employees, there is joint ownership of the mission.

All employees need to be encouraged to take the initiative with regard to ethics issues. Open-door policies and whistle blowing (if required) should be supported. A compelling business case can bolster enthusiasm for this sort of ethics partnership, going a long way toward persuading management that ethics is a first-priority business need. Involvement and ownership require that programs be personalized for people in various departments. Thus, *the fifth step* is to announce an ethics-partnership program that involves employees at all levels in the process of sharpening the ethical edge.

6. A common view that ethics is a cultural issue. When ethics is seen as a cultural issue, people focus on the environment as a potential source of competitive advantage.

It is a mistake to see ethics as a crusade to rout out evil in the organization, yet in many organizations, ethics comes under the purview of narrowly focused security units buried in the bowels of human resource departments and driven by a mission to catch the in-house bad guys. These security types are easily recognized by the handcuff tie-clips they proudly display. Of course, this is not ethics. Neither is ethics purely an accounting function to be handled by the internal audit department and the corporate secretary or legal affairs staff. Both of these mistaken views are typically found in level 1.0 and level 2.0 firms. The more-progressive level 3.0 firms tend to see ethics as a human resource function. Level 4.0 and level 5.0 firms broaden the scope to include leaders: the CEO directs the ethics program and implementation is every executive's job, regardless of division. "Ethics management" in the level 5.0 firm is a line function as well as a staff function. Some ethical exemplars even have trained ethicists in the boardrooms helping to guide the organization into the future. Thus, *the sixth step* is to create a set of norms that influence ethical behavior.

This step can be initiated by appointing an ethics advisor or an ethics ombudsman who reports to the CEO or to the board. The company should make an annual practice of conducting an "ethics audit" as well. To this we may add a note of caution. Simply making an appointment won't change the culture. The key is CEO *ownership* of the issue and *follow-up*, with everyone in the ranks, through training, codes, and recognition of ethical behavior in the reward systems. For example, at Dinotar, a performance bonus is determined in part by an employee's ability to eliminate time lost due to accidents. At Gannett, bonuses are tied in part to success in meeting goals for hiring women and minorities.

7. Procedures and systems that ensure that ethics is a central part of selection and performance management. When values and ethics are central to selection, training, and performance management, there is more congruence between what the organization says it's about and the values that people really hold.

It may be a tired maxim, but it's true: people do what they are rewarded for. In this respect, when organizational and personal values become more closely aligned, the rewards evolve synergistically. The organization is rewarded by the commitment people have to it, and people are rewarded by the trust and value the organization assigns to them. This congruence does not just occur accidentally. The organization needs constant infusions in the form of . . .

— new people,

— enhanced training programs,

— up-to-date rewards and recognition processes,

— key positions filled from without *and* from within.

These infusions are constructive to the extent that they reinforce the importance of values in all business transactions. The best way to create an ethical culture is to recruit and retain people who reflect the values and principles of the corporate culture. Thus, *the seventh step* is to review the selection, training, and performance management systems to ensure that adequate attention is given and sound measures are available to tighten the fit between organizational and personal values.

8. Tailored education and training programs. When education and training programs are tailored to the needs of the target population, people are able to apply their skills in creative and productive ways.

Conducting such programs independently of the other action steps discussed here would be an exercise in futility. However, when they are made a central part of a well-orchestrated process to achieve an ethical edge, they serve a critical purpose. Ideally, we should see ethics as a functional application of productive thinking and relating.[1,2] Traditionally, new-employee orientation, management seminars, and decision-making courses address the issues of ethics, but most of this training is geared toward compliance issues. Thus, *the eighth step* is (a) to determine what level of ethics your education and training programs are designed to achieve, and (b) to decide if that intervention is consistent with your goals. Ultimately, the education and training efforts should produce thinking managers who relate constructively.

9. Multiple upward and downward communication channels. With such channels, employees feel informed about what's going on and free to initiate their ideas for improvement.

Multiple communication vehicles and channels give employees confidence that ethical issues can be addressed. They need to believe that there are people in the organization who will hear their ideas for creating an ethical edge. One way to facilitate upward communication is, as mentioned earlier, to create ethics advisors and ombudsman whose job is to respond to employee ideas, suggestions, and concerns. In most organizations, there are a variety of vehicles for downward communications, but one effective ethics strategy is to roll out the training from the top, using managers as trainers. This reinforces the importance of ethics, provides the opportunity to integrate ethics into business operations, and enables managers to personalize key principles in their respective units. Thus, *the ninth step* is to explore options for expanding upward and downward communication. Leaders cannot merely impose ethics from on high; they have to find out from associates and colleagues exactly what is going on "down there."

10. Broad monitoring of ethics goals. When progress toward ethical goals is closely monitored, sustained action is more likely to occur.

The broad monitoring of such goals enables executives to establish baseline data, observe trends over time, and set appropriate goals. The appendix of this book provides an ethics-assessment and goal-setting instrument with a rating system for a comprehensive evaluation of ethical possibilities. The instrument should be used by an internal audit committee or external consultant to monitor progress on a regular basis. Thus, *the tenth step* is to monitor progress on your initiatives so that you can sustain your ethical edge.

STRATEGIES FOR ACCOUNTABILITY

Ethical leadership must also be viewed from the perspective of accountability. A number of strategies in this area have been articulated by Fred Bird, a professor of religion at Montreal's Concordia University and a leading authority on business ethics. There are seven strategies in all:

1. Legal accountability

2. Market accountability

3. Union accountability

4. Special interest and professional association accountability

5. Board of Directors accountability

6. Policy accountability

7. Stakeholder accountability

1. Legal accountability. Legislation is becoming pro-lific and increasingly severe. Governments around the globe are enacting and enforcing more and more laws related to the way businessmen deal with people, cus-tomers, and their communities. In the area of environment, new regulations demand high sensitivity to the concept of sustainable development. Essentially, ethical leaders need to make a choice. Do they spend exorbitant amounts of money trying to lower compliance thresholds by lobbying government to relax legislation? Do they invest in meas-ures that ensure that their organizations go beyond compli-ance? Or do they try to create an ethical edge by taking a leadership position in ethics?

General Motors took the first road. It spent $1.8 billion over the last decade lobbying against enhanced clean-air leg-islation. However, as we have seen in this book, several com-panies have profited by taking the high road.

2. Market accountability. Investors, purchasers, and job applicants are expanding the list of values and criteria on which they make buying decisions. Business ethics appear regularly on those lists. And "ethics monitors" are making information on companies' standard business practices more available. Leaders will need to know how their compa-nies stack up against the competition on ethical criteria as well as product quality. Just as quality was the driving force of the 1980s, ethics will be the driving force of the new mil-lennium. Organizations such as the New York–based Council for Economic Priorities are likely to heighten scrutiny and pressure.

3. Union accountability. Over the years, unions have helped to redefine and thus enhance ethical practices in busi-ness. Unions continue to exert pressure on companies to ensure fair employee treatment and safe working conditions. Historically, unions have had a narrow focus at the bargain-ing table. Their traditional targets are fair wages, safe work-ing conditions, and health and pension benefits. If unions decide to expand their scope to include issues related to corporate culture, customer relationships, and community responsibility, they may regain the strength they have lost in recent years. The question is, *Who will seize the initiative to capture the hearts and minds of the people?*

4. Special interest and professional association accountability. People have loyalties that go beyond their organizations. Most employees belong to at least one special-interest group (such as a religious denomination, Greenpeace, Amnesty International) or professional association (such as in engineering, medicine, marketing) that has a defined set of values. These values exert a powerful influence on behavior. When corporate values run counter to them, employees will act according to the values with which they most personally identify.

5. Board of Directors accountability. Boards increasingly perceive themselves as "moral assessors." Part of their role is to ensure ethical conduct of the businesses they direct or advise. As this change in their perceived role takes hold, senior management will get a new message: upward movement and ethical conduct are intimately tied. And standards of ethical conduct will be applied to the aspiring executive's influence on the culture, people, customers, and communities with which the organization leads.

6. Policy accountability. Ethical leaders do more than spew out policies and procedures. They write and say the right words, but more importantly, they do the right things. Policies should include statements about what kind of culture the organization wants to create, how it wants to treat its employees and its customers, and how it wants to relate to the community. These policies must be audited and measured with tools similar to the scales provided throughout this book and in the appendix. Codes of ethics, standards of business conduct, and corporate communications need to be reinforced with sign-offs on understanding and rewards for ethical action.

7. Stakeholder accountability. You cannot rely exclusively on directives coming down from on high; you need to encourage people to speak up. Ethical leaders urge people to express their concerns, and don't hold candor against them; thus they create a culture of openness. Ethical leaders also institute several mechanisms to facilitate an upward flow of information—they not only set the tone, but listen to the pulse. And they serve as resources to their people. Accountability requires open communication, where people see themselves as stakeholders with the business.

These principles, action steps, and strategies can be simplified by following the brief implementation outline below:

1. Get a general sense of where you are by studying the scales provided in the overview sections of Chapters 1 through 4.

2. Decide where you want to be as an organization.

3. If you rated yourself less than 3.0 on certain areas, review the chapter sections on those areas to develop specific plans to get to level 3.0.

4. If you rated yourself 3.0 or more on certain areas, review the chapter sections that discuss the "possibilities" realized by ethical exemplars in those areas. Decide what your organization can do to match or exceed the outcomes achieved by these exemplars.

5. Put these questions on your staff-meeting agenda on a regular basis:

   • How can we create a more ethical culture within our organization?

   • What are the current obstacles or problems that stand in our way?

   • What possibilities might open up for us if we develop an ethical edge?

REFERENCES

1. Carkhuff, R. R. *Interpersonal Skills and Human Productivity.* Amherst, Massachusetts: HRD Press, 1983.
2. Carkhuff, R. R. *The Exemplar.* Amherst, Massachusetts: HRD Press, 1989.

•••••••••

Summary

At this point you might be saying, "Well, it all sounds good, but . . .

- is this just another bandwagon?

- is this going to result in a mass confessional?

- is this going to cost more than it's worth?

- are resources available?"

Ethics is not just another bandwagon. Ethical leadership has one outcome: sustainable development. We cannot sustain progress if our corporate culture does not support our policies. We cannot sustain growth if we do not invest in our people and treat them as whole persons with unique gifts. We cannot sustain profits if we fail to help our customers achieve their productivity and profitability goals. We cannot sustain development on a global basis if we do not treat the

environment more respectfully and help transform developing countries into healthier, productive, and more prosper-
ous communities.

Ethical leadership does not mean mass confessions. It does
not involve finding a guiding light or forming a new business religion. Quite the contrary. Ethical leadership is not
interested in lies — it seeks the truth. Ethical leadership is not
interested in myths — it demands realities. Ethical leadership is not hardhearted — it is softhearted, but tough-
minded.

Winning the right way does not cost more than it's worth. It can
be expensive: For example, investing in conservation and recycling might require substantial cash outlays in the early stages
because educating people about these things costs money.
Insisting on product safety and customer benefits requires further expenses. However, the cost of trying to win without an
extraordinary scrutiny of ethics can be disastrous. For an illustration of the consequences of ethical sloppiness, we have only
to look at Union Carbide's complicity in the Bhopal tragedy
and Johns-Manville's slow decline into bankruptcy over prod-
uct-liability lawsuits arising from asbestos-related health
problems. And as we saw in Chapter 4: Winning for the
Community, the costs of delaying intervention usually out-
weigh the costs of taking immediate initiative.

It is very difficult to quantify damage-control costs, not
the least because cost figures are highly dependent on the
control strategy. However, in the eastern United States, it has
been estimated that cutting in half the remaining sulphur
dioxide emission from existing sources would cost $5 billion
per year, increasing electricity rates by two to three percent;
and materials-corrosion damage due to CO_2 emissions is estimated to cost $7 billion annually in 17 states in the United
States.[1] Thousands of waste disposal sites exist, but many of
them are likely to require some form of remedial action.
Cleanup is expensive — estimates range from $10 billion for
West Germany to $100 billion for the United States — but the

health risks of continued contamination far exceed the amounts quoted here.[2]

Resources are available but require redistribution. Committing funds to clean up past abuses and to prevent future disasters will require a redistribution of resources. Government, for instance, will need to shift allocation of funds from other areas, such as the military, to the environment. President Eisenhower observed at the end of his term in office that "every gun that is made, every warship launched, every rocket fired represents in the final analysis a theft from those who hunger and are not fed, who are cold and are not clothed."[3]

The world spent at least $1 trillion on military goods and services in 2002, or more than $2.5 billion a day, up sharply since the September 11 attacks. The real cost is what the same resources might otherwise be used for. For example:

- An action plan for tropical forests would cost an estimated $1.3 billion a year.

- A United Nations action plan for reversing the desertification process would cost $4.5 billion a year.

- The United Nations' Water and Sanitation Decade, designed to provide clean water for household use in the Third World, would cost $30 billion per year.

- The supply of contraceptive materials to all women already motivated to use family planning would cost $1 billion per year.[4]

Ethical leaders need not feel lonely. There are people throughout the world working on these issues. Here are some recommended sources:

United States:

Ethics Resource Center
1025 Connecticut Ave., NW
Suite 1003
Washington, D.C. 20036
202-223-3411

Council on Economic Priorities
30 Irving Place
New York, N.Y. 10003
212-420-1133

Canada:

EthicScan Canada, Ltd. and the Canadian Clearinghouse
   for Consumer and Corporate Ethics
P.O. Box 165, Postal Station 'S'
Toronto, Ontario M5M 4L7
416-783-6776

REFERENCES

1. *World Commission on Environment and Development. Our Common Future.* Oxford: Oxford University Press, 1987.
2. Ibid.
3. Ibid.
4. Ibid.

Appendix A
An ETHICS Evaluation Tool

ETHICS ASSESSMENT AND GOAL-SETTING

Evaluation Tool for Human and
Information Capital Support (ETHICS)

Directions: Rate your organization from 1 to 5 on the following dimensions of ethical leadership; then check your responses to the scoring key that follows.

CULTURE

1. Creating a Vision

- ❑ **5.0** — See the world as your community
- ❑ **4.0** — See the nation as your community
- ❑ **3.0** — See your customers as your community
- ❑ **2.0** — See your employee population as part of your community
- ❑ **1.0** — Don't see the importance of community

2. Defining Values

- ❑ **5.0** — All major decisions evaluated on values
- ❑ **4.0** — Values communicated and modeled
- ❑ **3.0** — Well-defined set of values
- ❑ **2.0** — Loosely defined set of values
- ❑ **1.0** — Undefined values

3. Embedding Norms

- ❑ **5.0** — Culture rewards ethical business practices
- ❑ **4.0** — Culture encourages ethical business practices
- ❑ **3.0** — Culture supports ethical business practices
- ❑ **2.0** — Culture accepts unethical business practices
- ❑ **1.0** — Culture encourages unethical business practices

Continued

PEOPLE

4. Developing Employees

- ❏ **5.0** — Increase street value
- ❏ **4.0** — Functional applications
- ❏ **3.0** — General skills
- ❏ **2.0** — Concepts (programs without skills)
- ❏ **1.0** — Facts

5. Promoting Health and Safety

- ❏ **5.0** — Culture change
- ❏ **4.0** — Personal development
- ❏ **3.0** — Physical risk reduction
- ❏ **2.0** — First Aid, primary care
- ❏ **1.0** — Full responsibility on employee

6. Supporting Balance

- ❏ **5.0** — On-site day care and full range of family-care benefits
- ❏ **4.0** — Subsidized day care and selected family-care benefits
- ❏ **3.0** — Computerized referral service for family care
- ❏ **2.0** — Recognition of changing needs
- ❏ **1.0** — Demand traditional roles and/or ignore changing trends

7. Valuing Differences

- ❏ **5.0** — Meaningful board and senior-management representation of minorities and women (inclusivity)
- ❏ **4.0** — Aggressive support for internal promotion of women and minorities
- ❏ **3.0** — Affirmative Action policy that is used

Continued

❑ **2.0** — Equal Employment Opportunity (EEO)

❑ **1.0** — No representation or intent of representation (exclusivity)

CUSTOMERS

8. Connecting Ethics with Product Development

❑ **5.0** — Ethics drive decisions

❑ **4.0** — Ethics are an integral part of decisions

❑ **3.0** — Ethics influence decisions

❑ **2.0** — Ethics are considered in decisions

❑ **1.0** — Ethics are not considered in decisions

9. Connecting Ethics with Marketing

❑ **5.0** — Interdependent relationships

❑ **4.0** — Customer productivity

❑ **3.0** — Customer benefits

❑ **2.0** — Customer satisfaction

❑ **1.0** — Customer manipulation

10. Connecting Ethics with Manufacturing

❑ **5.0** — Processes create meaningful work

❑ **4.0** — Processes ensure employee and environmental health

❑ **3.0** — Processes are safe

❑ **2.0** — Processes do not degrade the environment

❑ **1.0** — Processes degrade the environment

Continued

COMMUNITIES

11. Enhancing the Environment

☐ **5.0** — Environmental leadership

☐ **4.0** — Community outreach

☐ **3.0** — Environmental protection

☐ **2.0** — Compliance

☐ **1.0** — Staying out of Trouble

12. Contributing to Community Resources

☐ **5.0** — More than 3 percent of pre-tax profit

☐ **4.0** — 3 percent of pre-tax profit

☐ **3.0** — 2 percent of pre-tax profit

☐ **2.0** — 1 percent of pre-tax profit

☐ **1.0** — Less than 1 percent of pre-tax profit

13. Participating in Community Organizations

☐ **5.0** — Community involvement rewarded, particularly when it contributes to the creation of productive communities

☐ **4.0** — Community involvement encouraged, with an emphasis on sustainable development

☐ **3.0** — Community involvement recognized/supported

☐ **2.0** — Community involvement accepted

☐ **1.0** — Community involvement discouraged

➥ *Now go on to the Scoring Key . . .*

SCORING KEY:
ETHICS ASSESSMENT AND GOAL-SETTING

Culture

1. Creating a Vision

5.0: The organization sees the world as its community, and sees potential for gain or loss in terms of the world community. Level 5.0 organizations strive to achieve full interdependence; believe in open sharing of information; believe in universal connectivity; and work on sustainable-development projects.

4.0: The organization sees its "location" as part of its community. It understands the civic responsibility of corporations.

3.0: The organization sees the customer as an important part of its community. It sees potential for interdependent gain or loss.

2.0: The organization sees the employees as part of its community, but it also sees potential for gain or loss only inwardly.

1.0: The company does not see itself connected to any community. It sees potential for gain or loss entirely in individualistic management and/or stockholder terms.

2. Defining Values

5.0: All major decisions are evaluated on values. The values are weighted and considered as a whole. There is great resistance in the organization to making single-value decisions.

4.0: The organization communicates its values and models them. People understand what the organization is about.

3.0: The organization has a well-defined set of values. These values are probably published and framed and may even show up in the annual reports. People at lower levels in the organization, however, don't hear about them or see them practiced.

2.0: The organization would say it has a set of values, but everyone would define them differently. Activities are independent of value.

1.0: The organization has no values that define it in any way. It is totally opportunistic.

3. Embedding Norms

5.0: The organization rewards ethical practices. For example, promotions are based, in part, on the way employees treat people, customers, and the community.

4.0: The organization encourages ethical practices. For example, employees who want to participate in community activities are given the time to do so.

3.0: The organization supports ethical practices. People could say, "Around here, people try to win the right way."

2.0: The organization accepts unethical practices. If people are caught stealing or engaging in fraud, the offenses are often overlooked.

1.0: The organization encourages unethical business practices. The "robber baron" mentality characterizes these types of organizations.

To review the above, see Chapter 1: Creating an Ethical Culture.

People

4. Developing Employees

5.0: The organization trains its employees so that their street value meets or exceeds their compensation in their current job. By so doing, the organization reduces employees' fears about instability, insecurity, and reductions in force because the employees know they can leave whenever the gap between their personal values and their job requirements is too large. What employees may lose in job security, they will gain in career security. And, at the same time, this type of psychological contract eliminates the pressure on employers to make lifetime employment guarantees. At level 5.0, the ethical organization is free to achieve a realistic balance between satisfying worker values and meeting stakeholder recommendations. Both the organization and the individual win through improved education.

4.0: The generic skills are reinforced with opportunities to learn and practice functional applications (for example: coaching, delegating, and conducting performance reviews).

3.0: Employees are equipped with an educational core set of skills designed to help them think better, relate more constructively, and plan systematically. These skills empower employees to contribute to the organization.

2.0: Employees are offered programs that give them a conceptual overview of their job, its function, the skills required to perform the job, and how those skills contribute to the organization.

1.0: Employees are given only the facts they need to know in order to do their jobs.

5. Promoting Health and Safety

5.0: The organization's focus is to create an environment that supports positive safety and health practices. The emphasis is on culture change and building health partnerships between the individual and the organization. At level 5.0, both the organization and the individual win. The organization gains through a more energetic, enthusiastic, and creative work force. And the individual benefits through improved health, vitality, and career fulfillment.

4.0: The organization supports personal development through a variety of interventions designed to help employees improve their physical, emotional, and intellectual well-being. For example, these programs may include fitness, nutrition, interpersonal communication, self-esteem, managing change, and creative thinking.

3.0: The organization sponsors an array of programs on accident prevention and physical risk reduction. These may include smoking cessation, high-blood-pressure control, cholesterol reduction, stress management, and weight control. Such programs are aimed at preventing loss due to sickness or absence.

2.0: The organization provides first aid and basic primary care. The idea here is to treat workplace injuries on site to increase speed of response, provide convenient service, and reduce the time employees are off the job obtaining medical assistance.

1.0: The organization puts full responsibility for health and safety on the employee. There is no attempt to distribute the responsibility appropriately and take commensurate action with that distribution.

6. Supporting Balance

5.0: The organization is sensitive and responsive to a full range of family and personal needs. On-site day care is provided, leaves of absence are granted for family and personal issues, and elder-care needs are understood and supported. Overall, the corporate culture encourages a healthy balance between family and career and treats employees as whole persons.

4.0: Organizations provide subsidies for child care and offer selected benefits related to family issues. These organizations encourage people to pursue personal interests.

3.0: Organizations have some support services available in the form of computerized referral or personal counseling for employees to find assistance for family-related issues.

2.0: Organizations recognize the changing needs of the work force and the changing roles of men and women. In these organizations, policies usually reflect some sensitivity to parenting and elder-care issues, and allow for generous leaves of absence for issues as they arise.

1.0: Organizations demand traditional roles and/or ignore changing trends. In these organizations, there are different expectations for women than for men and there is great resistance to any efforts to support changing roles. Also, these organizations typically leave little room for family needs and are not supportive when issues arise in families from birth or adoption through to illness or death.

7. Valuing Differences

5.0: There is meaningful representation of women and minorities among senior management staff and on the board. These organizations see involvement of women and minorities as essential for business success and *in no way* engage merely in token efforts to satisfy public relations goals or government guidelines.

4.0: There is aggressive support for internal promotions of women and minorities and evidence of that support on the board and in executive offices. In these organizations, differences are not only valued, but seen as gifts.

3.0: Organizations have and use Affirmative Action policy. These organizations actively hire and promote women and members of minority groups for management positions.

2.0: Organizations at least have an EEO policy that states the intention of the company to broaden its leadership representation to women and minorities. These organizations recognize that they need to involve their constituents in the management of the business.

1.0: White male dominance in the board room and executive suites is widely evident. These organizations attempt to maintain the status quo by hiring and promoting from within the "old boy" network.

To review the above, see Chapter 2: Winning through People.

Customers

8. Connecting Ethics with Product Development

5.0: Product development is driven by ethical issues. In these organizations, the first question is, "What are the major issues our world faces?" And the next question is, "What products or services can we develop to help solve those issues and still achieve our profit objectives?"

4.0: Ethics and decision making are integrally related. In these organizations, if a new product or service does not meet the highest standards of business conduct, it is not introduced.

3.0: Ethical issues are an important part of the "gate" process. In these organizations, new products or services must pass a basic "ethics test" before they are introduced.

2.0: Ethical questions are entertained in the product "gate-review" process, but the emphasis is clearly more technology-driven than people-driven.

1.0: Products are engineered without thought about their impact on people. In these organizations, the only question is, "What can we sell?"

9. Connecting Ethics with Marketing

5.0: Marketing efforts revolve around interdependence. At this level, organizations are empowered to openly share information so that all of them may become productive and profitable. This kind of interdependent marketing requires openness and authenticity. The implication is that the producer will help the consumer make the best possible choice, even if that means not choosing the producer's product — the ultimate ethical position. This, of course, raises the question, "Where is the ethical edge in this construct? It sounds like I could only lose." The answer is rhetorical: "With the kind of relationship established through this approach, who else will the consumer turn to?"

4.0: Marketing efforts are designed to show how products or services contribute to improvements in actual customer productivity. The subtle distinction between benefits and added productivity rests in the ability of the producer to understand the customer's frame of reference and his or her particular needs. Level 4.0 organizations encourage their employees to immerse themselves in the customer's business in order to establish better relationships with clients and understand their specific needs. Theoretically, this immersion enables the producer to tailor products and services to given needs.

3.0: Marketing is aimed toward real customer benefits. At this level, organizations attempt to fill a niche by demonstrating how the client will benefit from their product or service.

2.0: Marketing is aimed toward customer satisfaction. Emphasis is on a product quality independent of benefit (for example, much of food-advertising efforts fall into this category).

1.0: Marketing is seen as any way to manipulate the customer to buy a product or service independent of the ethics involved or the benefits provided. Good examples of level-1.0 marketing include the home-video purchase approach, in which enthusiastic salespersons hype a variety of products that consumers can purchase from home by calling a toll-free number. Lotteries would also fall into this category.

10. Connecting Ethics with Manufacturing

5.0: Manufacturing processes are designed to create meaningful work for employees. At this level, organizations do what they can to involve employees in decisions and to empower them to act. Employees have opportunities to learn new skills, and supervisors get the training required to engage employees in productive dialogue, to build high-performing teams, and to collaborate with employees to solve problems.

4.0: Manufacturing processes are designed to ensure the health of employees and the environment. At this level, organizations employ ergonomics consultants to reduce the incidents of repetitive-strain injuries and environmental consultants to eliminate risks related to hazardous materials and toxic chemicals. The organization also provides exercise breaks, rest breaks, and health-promotion opportunities.

3.0: Manufacturing processes are safe. At this level, companies employ safety experts and have well-defined procedures and training programs designed to prevent accidents. Investments are made in the work environment to reduce risks from noise, heat, light, and air pollution.

2.0: Manufacturing processes do not degrade the environment. At this level, the company takes care to properly dispose of hazardous wastes and takes whatever steps are necessary to avoid air pollution. Compliance is taken seriously.

1.0: Manufacturing processes degrade the environment. At this level, organizations simply do what they need to do to avoid getting into too much trouble independent of the detrimental effects on the environment.

To review the above, see Chapter 3: Winning with Customers.

Community

11. Enhancing the Environment

5.0: The organization takes a leadership role in reducing pollutants, managing waste, or reducing chlorofluorocarbons (CFCs).

4.0: Organizations make sure that communities are informed of any toxic chemicals that could be released into the air or water. Efforts are made to curtail air or water pollution, to recycle materials, to conserve energy as best as possible, to include environmentally sensitive landscaping and re-vegetation in all building projects, and to avoid billboard advertising.

3.0: The company takes a proactive approach to environmental issues. It ensures that all hazardous materials are properly managed, that indoor air quality for its employees is acceptable, and that all waste is properly managed.

2.0: The organization meets the letter of the law. For example, it complies with U.S. environmental legislation such as Sara Title III.

1.0: The company's goal is simply to stay out of trouble. In these organizations, managers will say, "If I don't hear about it and I don't see any obvious disasters, we are doing our job."

12. Contributing to Community Resources

The scale is self-explanatory, but it may be helpful to see how many corporations in selected cities meet the level 3.0 or level 5.0 goal. The following chart shows the number of corporations in five cities that have joined the two-percent or five-percent giving club. Membership in this club means that organizations pledge a certain percentage of their pre-tax earnings to charity.

	2 Percent	5 Percent
Minneapolis	33	71
Kansas City	107	?
Baltimore	?	53
San Francisco	50	?
Seattle	143	?

13. Participating in Community Organizations

5.0: The organization is committed to creating productive communities in which interdependent relationships are established among homes, schools, community organizations, and businesses.

4.0: The organization's investment and resource decisions are all considered in terms of sustainable development: Will the organization's actions have positive, long-term, environmental, and economic effects on the community? These organizations encourage constructive community involvement.

3.0: Partnership relationships with the host community are encouraged. The community is seen as a resource for talented people, so all parties benefit from effective community development. Thus, employee involvement is recognized and supported.

2.0: Host communities are seen as places where "friendly" relationships are advantageous to business because they can lead, for instance, to favorable zoning decisions. These organizations therefore accept employee involvement in community organizations as long as it does not take away from time on the job.

1.0: Host communities are seen only as places to set up shop. Employees are discouraged from participating in any community organization. In these organizations, there is disregard for the community consequences of business practices.

To review the above, see Chapter 4: Winning for the Community.

Appendix B

DEBATE AND GUIDANCE:

THE LITERATURE AND

BEST PRACTICES

The public debate on ethics is not new. In the fourth century B.C., the Greek philosopher Plato explored justice and the good society in his *Republic*, thus initiating the inquiry of how to integrate ethical principles in a rational context. Twenty-four centuries and thousands of books later, Paul Tillich in 1952 wrote of the inextricable link between being and courage and examined the basic human challenges and opportunities for growth and ethical being.[1] Fifteen years later, Robert K. Greenleaf wrote a powerful book, *Servant Leadership*, based on the idea that becoming a great leader requires seeing oneself first as a servant.[2] This journey into the nature of legitimate power and greatness demonstrates how a servant-leader must be both visionary and realistic.

The above three examples represent numerous published works that offer us thoughtful discourses on and significant guidance in ethical leadership. A chronological list of more-recent works, drawn from Grace and Skelton's *100 Top Readings for Ethical Leaders*,[3] is provided below along with brief commentary.

- **1987: Kouzes and Posner, *The Leadership Challenge: How to Get Extraordinary Things Done in Organizations*.**[4] In this book, the authors overview the five leadership practices common to successful leaders: challenging the process, inspiring a shared vision, enabling others to act, modeling the way, and encouraging the heart. The first and last principles speak volumes to the leaders in today's corporations. Who was challenging the process at Enron and WorldCom when proposals were made to capitalize operating expenses or hide expenses in offshore holding companies? Who was encouraging the heart when employees were asked to keep purchasing company stock, even as leaders braced for impending disasters?

- **1989: Badaracco and Ellsworth, *Leadership and the Quest for Integrity*.**[5] The authors, associates of Harvard Business School, pose leadership dilemmas and how the resolution of those dilemmas requires a continuous quest for consistency among personal beliefs, organizational vision, and individual behavior. I wonder if Martha Stewart confronted this dilemma when she sold her shares of IMClone stock?

- **1990: Gardner, *On Leadership*.**[6] This book explores the nature of leadership and issues of morality and power in the context of community. Leadership concepts such as long-term thinking, looking at the whole, and influencing beyond boundaries are suggested as critical to success. Where was the long-term thinking at Xerox when leaders decided to misrepresent revenues over a period of several years in order to meet Wall Street's quarterly expectations?

- **1990: Peter Senge,** *The Fifth Discipline: The Art and Practice of the Learning Organization.*[7] Cambridge, Massachusetts was the central source of several great constructs in 1990. While Howard Gardner was describing effective leadership at Harvard, Peter Senge created the fifth discipline at MIT. Here he predicts that the organizations bound to excel in the future are those that master how to tap people's commitment and capacity to learn. It appears from recent allegations that discipline was missing in action from many companies accused of unethical behavior. And there is nothing more damaging to employee commitment and capacity than learning that the company for which you work is accused of a scandal.

- **1992: Bryson and Crosby,** *Leadership for the Common Good: Tackling Public Problems in a Shared Power World.*[8] The authors propose a number of ideas for sharing power and ensuring that a diversity of voices and needs are heard. In my experience with corporations, it has always been a challenge to get leaders to see the advantages of sharing power and seeking out multiple sources of input. I wonder how many of the scandals that are currently plaguing corporate America could have been prevented if leaders had tapped a wider and deeper range of thoughts and feelings.

- **1993: Barrantine,** *When the Canary Stops Singing: Women's Perspectives on Transforming Business.*[9] Barrantine describes a transformation in business related to the need for more humane and nurturing

workplaces, more balance and harmony, and more
interdependence and community. It is my belief that we
need more women in executive roles in corporations. I
wonder what the demographics looked like in the companies that are currently accused of unethical behavior.

- **1993: Block,** *Stewardship: Choosing Service over Self-
Interest.*[10] Block suggests there is a need for a fundamental change in the way we govern our organizations.
He defines stewardship as accepting ownership and
accountability for the well-being of the larger organization. There is no question that insatiable self-interest has
caused an unfair distribution of power and wealth that
has not well-served our organizations or our world.

- **1993: O'Toole,** *The Executive's Compass: Business and
the Good Society.*[11] O'Toole, the moderator for the
Aspen Institute's Executive Seminar, suggests that the
most difficult issues confronting leaders are often
rooted in social, political, and economic value differences. It appears that the current corporate compass is
pointing in the wrong direction. Maybe we need a new
set of guideposts to chart our way.

- **1993: Ray and Rinzler,** *The New Paradigm in Business:
Emerging Strategies for Leadership and Organizational
Change.*[12] Ray and Rinzler observe that leadership
occurs within a multicultural workplace, and that business must take a larger social and environmental
responsibility for its actions. They suggest that business
needs to put people and creativity at the center of the
work world. While I agree with these observations and
suggestions, I don't see a lot of evidence that we are
making progress on these fronts.

- **1993: Reyes and Perreault, "Wholeness and Council: A
Native American Perspective on Leadership."**[13] In
this article, the authors draw on the values of the Native

American culture to give insights into leadership and focus on the importance of wholeness and authenticity. They suggest that leadership should build community rather than rely upon hierarchy, personality, or dominance. History will record that we have not only abused and cheated our Native American brothers and sisters, but also cheated ourselves by ignoring this great source of wisdom. We could learn a great deal from Native American beliefs about community.

- **1993: Terry, *Authentic Leadership: Courage into Action*.**[14] The author claims that the central organizing principle of leadership is authenticity. He suggests that leadership depends on the ability to frame issues correctly and then to call forth an authentic action in response to the issues this identifies. I don't know how a leader can be ethical without being authentic. Ethical leadership means doing what you say, saying what you do, and saying to others what you say to yourself. These euphemisms translate fairly directly into "Don't lie." Clearly, the ethical aberrations that occurred recently all involve lies of one sort or another.

- **1994: Chrislip and Larson, *Collaborative Leadership: How Citizens and Civic Leaders Can Make a Difference*.**[15] In this book, the authors posit that in an increasingly complex society, citizens and civic leaders need to exhibit leadership based on constructive collaboration. They suggest that effective leaders are democratic and inclusive, inherently believing that people can work together to address their needs. I have personally seen the power of such an approach in my work with New Jersey's Somerset Hills YMCA, where I served as Chairman of the Board from 1985 to 1988 and continue to serve on the Advisory Board. This YMCA is an exemplar of collaborative leadership in the community. Bob Lamauro, the CEO of the YMCA, created the

Unity Community program, which involves citizens from all aspects of life in a collaborative effort to transcend all boundaries and provide more-effective services to all members of the community. It is truly a model program that demonstrates how leaders can make a difference.

- **1994: Fox, *The Reinvention of Work: A New Vision of Livelihood for Our Time.*[16]** Here Fox discusses how life and livelihood are integrated with spirit to achieve a life of depth, meaning, and purpose along with contribution to the greater community. Leaders need to create meaningful work environments for their colleagues and serve as "soul models" who make this vision a reality in their organizations.

- **1994: Heifitz, *Leadership Without Easy Answers.*[17]** In this book, Heifitz examines the theory and practice of leadership in the context of an uncertain economy and rising social issues. Clearly, this century has ushered in a plethora of social issues in a terribly uncertain economy. Death from AIDS is expected to triple to 60 million people by 2020. Violence violates any semblance of peaceful harmony on a daily basis. No, there are no easy answers, but there are new ways of thinking and relating that could make a difference in individual and organizational life.

- **1995: Conger, "Moved by the Spirit: Leadership and Spirituality in the Workplace."[18]** In a vein similar to Heifitz, Conger argues that we need a new state of mind and a new state of heart to foster human development and community spirit in our workplaces.

- **1995: Gardner, *Leading Minds: An Anatomy of Leadership.*[19]** Here Gardner takes a human-development and cognitive look at leadership, identifying the leader's mind as a crucial component of leadership. He emphasizes the concept of story, arguing that effective leaders create new stories. We need new stories in corporate America. We need stories of people who understand and appreciate the interconnected web of all existence. We need stories of leaders who have a new vision of what work and life might be. We need stories of people who want to make a difference and do.

- **1995: Sullivan, Work and Integrity:** *The Crisis and Promise of Professionalism in America.*[20] The author suggests that professional life needs to be restructured for technical competence, as well as civic awareness and purpose. I believe one-dimensional thinking is at the root of the unethical weed. We need to engage in multidimensional thinking and collaborative relating. We must think differently and relate differently if we are to have any hope of acting ethically and achieving the promise of professionalism.

- **1996: Jaworski,** *Synchronicity: The Inner Path of Leadership.*[21] The author argues that leadership is about wholeness and states that the leader's journey starts by looking inward and discovering the self. He believes that transformation requires three shifts in mind: how we see the world, how we understand relationships, and how we make commitments. In my 30 years of experience with leadership development, I have found there are five components of leadership that correspond well with Jaworski's suppositions. They are as follows:

  — Know and grow your own commitment and capabilities.

  — Know and grow others' commitment and capabilities.

  — Know and grow organizational capabilities.

- — Know and grow customers' commitment and capabilities.

- — Know and grow community commitment and capabilities.

- **1996: Kamungo and Mendonca, *Ethical Dimensions of Leadership*.**[22] In this book, the authors state that the vision, values, beliefs, and actions of the leader set the ethical tone and standards for the organization. In my experience with over 200 organizations, I have found that leadership role-modeling behavior is the most essential success factor for any culture-change effort. In order to create an ethical culture, organizational leaders must serve as role models; the reward system must reinforce ethical behavior; and there must be ongoing dialogue about how well the organization is institutionalizing desired norms and values.

- **2001: Johnson, *Meeting the Ethical Challenges of Leadership*.**[23] Johnson discusses the leader's character, the faces of evil, ethical standards and strategies, ethical decision-making formats, and shaping ethical contexts. He describes how a leader can build a culture of trust by stating core values and acting in accordance with those values.

- **2003: Paine, *Value Shift*.**[24] The author posits that corporate leaders need to go back to basics and adopt a qualitatively different kind of management. *Value Shift* suggests an approach that melds high ethical standards with outstanding business results. It articulates exactly why the superior performers of the future will be those companies that satisfy both the financial and social expectations of their constituencies. I believe Dr. Paine, a professor at the Harvard Business School, has made a significant contribution to the literature with this work.

She demonstrates clearly and powerfully how there is no conflict between the economic imperative and the ethical imperative.

REFERENCES

1. Tillich, P. *The Courage to Be.* New Haven, Connecticut: Yale University Press, 1952.
2. Greenleaf, R. K. *Servant Leadership: A Journey into the Nature of Legitimate Power and Greatness.* New York: Paulist Press, 1977.
3. Grace, W., and Skelton, C. *100 Top Readings for Ethical Leaders.* Seattle: Center for Ethical Leadership, 1998.
4. Kouzes, J., and Posner, B. *The Leadership Challenge: How to Get Extraordinary Things Done in Organizations.* San Francisco: Jossey-Bass, 1987.
5. Badaracco, J., and Ellsworth, R. *Leadership and the Quest for Integrity.* Boston: Harvard Business School Press, 1989.
6. Gardner, J. W. *On Leadership.* New York: The Free Press, 1990.
7. Senge, P. *The Fifth Discipline: The Art and Practice of the Learning Organization.* New York: Doubleday Currency, 1990.
8. Bryson, J., and Crosby, B. *Leadership for the Common Good: Tackling Public Problems in a Shared Power World.* San Francisco: Jossey-Bass, 1992.
9. Barrantine, P. *When the Canary Stops Singing: Women's Perspectives on Transforming Business.* San Francisco: Berrett-Koehler, 1993.
10. Block, P. *Stewardship: Choosing Service over Self-Interest.* San Francisco: Berrett-Koehler, 1993.
11. O'Toole, J. *The Executive's Compass: Business and the Good Society.* New York: Oxford University Press, 1993.
12. Ray, M., and Rinzler, A. *The New Paradigm in Business: Emerging Strategies for Leadership and Organizational Change.* New York: Jeremy P. Tarcher/Perigee, 1993.
13. Reyes, R., and Perreault, G. "Wholeness and Council: A Native American Perspective on Leadership." *Proteus: A Journal of Ideas,* 1993.
14. Terry, R. *Authentic Leadership: Courage into Action.* San Francisco: Jossey-Bass, 1993.
15. Chrislip, D., and Larson, C. *Collaborative Leadership: How Citizens and Civic Leaders Can Make a Difference.* San Francisco: Jossey-Bass, 1994.

16. Fox, M. *The Reinvention of Work: A New Vision of Livelihood for Our Time*: New York: Harper Collins, 1994.
17. Heifitz, R. *Leadership Without Easy Answers*. Cambridge, Massachusetts: Harvard University Press, 1994.
18. Conger, J. "Moved by the Spirit: Leadership and Spirituality in the Workplace." *OD Practitioner*, 27(1), 46–51, 1995.
19. Gardner, H. *Leading Minds: An Anatomy of Leadership*. New York: Basic Books, 1995.
20. Sullivan, W. *Work and Integrity: The Crisis and Promise of Professionalism in America*. New York: Harper Business, 1995.
21. Jaworski, J. *Synchronicity: The Inner Path of Leadership*. San Francisco: Berrett-Koehler, 1996.
22. Kamungo, R., and Mendonca, M. *Ethical Dimensions of Leadership*. Thousand Oaks, California: Sage Publications, 1996.
23. Johnson, C. *Meeting the Ethical Challenges of Leadership*. London: SAGE, 2001.
24. Paine, L. S. *Value Shift*. New York: McGraw-Hill, 2003.